UNITE

How to Bring Us Together and Lead Us to Greater Success

(with an Open Letter to President Biden <u>and</u> Subsequent Presidents)

John D. Correll

Fulfillment Press
U.S.A.

UNITE: How to Bring Us Together and Lead Us to Greater Success (with an Open Letter to President Biden <u>and</u> Subsequent Presidents)

Fulfillment Press | U.S.A.

Printed in United States of America
Paperback: ISBN: 978-1-938001-90-1
Hardcover: ISBN: 978-1-938001-91-8
Amazon URL: amazon.com/dp/1938001907
Version: TXT 2022-05-26 (13) | COV 2022-05-26 (4)
Fulfillment Press is an imprint and a dba of Correll Consulting, LLC
Front cover photo — Photographer John Correll. At a service station in
    Plymouth Twp, MI, February 21, 2019
Back cover photo — Photographer John Correll. At John Hancock
    Building in Chicago, 9:46 pm, July 26, 2018

Author information can be found at: correllconcepts.com/cv.pdf
(NOTE: this is not the same John Correll who creates the excellent
    children's books.)

Special thanks to Caitlyn, for providing initial positive feedback on the first draft of this book.

Special thanks to Janet and Lesley, for providing critiquing during the cover creation process.

Dedicated to Liam. May you always strive to become the finest person you're capable of being and to create the most beneficial life you're capable of creating and to help as many others as you can to do the same … and, as a result, derive Peace, Love, Joy, Meaning, Beauty, and Fulfillment throughout your life.

AN OPEN LETTER TO:

President Biden _and_ Subsequent Presidents, and _Also_ to All the Other Leaders in America

On November 7, 2020, shortly after the national election, President-elect Joe Biden said: _"With the campaign over, it's time to put the anger and the harsh rhetoric behind us and come together as a nation. It's time for America to unite. And to heal. We are the United States of America. And there's nothing we can't do, if we do it together."_

I want you — the reader of this book — to know that I'm one hundred percent behind that noble insight. But what have the Leaders in America done to bring us together? Honestly, I don't know. Still, I'm hoping and believing that it can happen, that it _will_ happen. So I reiterate: _"It's time to put the anger and the harsh rhetoric behind us and come together as a nation. It's time for America to unite. And to heal. We are the United States of America. And there's nothing we can't do, if we do it together."_

I'm hoping, I'm believing, that the Leaders in America — whoever you are, wherever you might be — truly desire to do what's needed to bring our nation together … and then, after that, do what's needed to enable us to become the finest nation we can be.

To that end I'm providing perspectives for your consideration. I've divided them into three parts. Part B (p. 10) tells what we must do to create _unity._ Part C (p. 64) describes how we can create _transcendence._ And, Part D (p. 118) is about enhancing _functionality._

I thank you in advance for reading this book and for doing all you can to help America to "unite and to heal" and to come together as a nation to accomplish great things.

My best regards,
John Correll — citizen

3

CONTENTS

UNITED
we stand,
DIVIDED
we fall.
— Patrick Henry, 1799

For our national leadership,
who should we be electing:
*(a) national unity **DESTROYERS***
<u>OR</u>
*(b) national unity **BUILDERS?***

More than any other factor,
how we act upon this question will
determine the future of our nation.

If we elect Unity Destroyers,
we will sink to our demise.

If, instead, we elect Unity <u>Builders</u>,
we will experience rising national
Functionality and Transcendence.

PART A:
Three Basic Precepts Required for Our Nation's Success

To succeed as a nation in years ahead, we must recognize and apply these three basic precepts:

1 – For most good things to come about, we need OPTIMAL FUNCTIONALITY of the Nation.

2 – For Optimal Functionality of the Nation, we need UNITY.

3 – To get Unity, we must inform our Leaders that creating Unity is a MANDATORY requirement of their job.

For clarity I define three terms.

Optimal functionality is: the capability to function in a way that achieves a certain desired outcome, such as, for example, a certain desired way of life.

Unity is: people working harmoniously together toward realization of common purpose and goals, such as, for example, the goal of realizing ongoing superlative improvement and life enhancement — a.k.a. transcendence.

Mandatory means: something that must be done in order for a person to keep their job.

Action Plan for Creating National Unity

ACTION 1: Make the Unity Movement apolitical — that is, design it and manage it in a way that avoids being exclusively aligned, or appearing to be exclusively aligned, with any particular party or person.

ACTION 2: Put emphasis on curtailing the major unity killers in America today. There are 20 such major unity killers. Each of them is clearly described in Part B of this book (p. 10).

ACTION 3: Put emphasis on the recognition and promotion of the Three Basic Precepts (cited on prior page).

ACTION 4: Establish at least one viable, strong government component (department, cabinet, committee, agency, or whatever) whose job is to (a) create mitigation of the 20 unity killers that are presently pervading our nation and (b) promote unity creation within our nation.

PART B: Creating Unity

Now this is *crucial.*

The critical first step to creating unity — or bringing our nation together — involves eliminating, or at least greatly curtailing, a group of unity-destroying elements that have been spreading like rampant cancer throughout our land. I dub them *unity killers.* There's twenty in all. For America to unite, these twenty sinister forces must be eliminated or at least greatly curtailed. Here they are:

1 – Negative Stereotyping
2 – Hate
3 – Vengeance
4 – Denigration
5 – Demonization
6 – Gloat
7 – Misrepresentation
8 – Propagandized News Reporting
9 – Chicken Little Fearmongering
10 – Variable Law Enforcement
11 – Hypocrisy
12 – Schadenfreude
13 – Deliberate Disrespecting
14 – One-side-only Characterization
15 – Subterfuge
16 – Group Extortion
17 – Genetic Sin Presupposition
18 – Political Gang Blackmail
19 – Radical Control Programs
20 - Superioration

This Part B describes those twenty unity killers.

Unity Killer #1:
Negative Stereotyping

To avoid any confusion, I start each of the twenty unity killer chapters by defining a key term that's used in the chapter.

So, as the term stereotyping is used here, a *stereotype* is: a simplistic, generalized description of a group of persons. Which means, **stereotyping** is: *the act of viewing or relating to an individual in a certain group as if they are an embodiment of a stereotype attached to that group.*

Stereotypes come in two forms: positive and negative. A stereotype that depicts a certain group in a positive light we call a *positive stereotype.* Conversely, a stereotype that depicts a certain group in a negative light we call a *negative stereotype.* So, the act of viewing or relating to an individual in a certain group as if they are an embodiment of a negative stereotype attached to that group we call *negative stereotyping.*

> **FROM HERE ON:** For simplicity, I'm no longer going to talk about positive stereotyping. So whenever the word "stereotyping" appears it's referring to the *negative* type of stereotyping.

Now here's the main point. Stereotyping almost always produces a negative outcome, and that outcome almost always includes discord, disdain, and disunity. It happens like this.

The first thing to know is that each person is unique — that is, they're a *unique individual* with a *unique life story.* This uniqueness is what defines them as a unique being; it's what makes them "special in all the world."

The second thing to know is: Deep down inside, nearly every person desires to <u>be</u> and to <u>feel</u> *unique and special.* This desire is so strong that, for this discussion, we're going to regard it as being a *basic* desire (need, want, drive) of most of humanity.

So, this is how stereotyping creates discord, disdain, and disunity.

When a person is subjected to stereotyping — that is, when they're being viewed or related to as a person who is an embodiment of a certain negative stereotype — it can create two counterproductive outcomes: (1) the impression and feeling that others are viewing them as being a *defective* person and (2) the impression and feeling that they're being viewed as a *non-unique* or *non-special* person or as "less than a full person."

So, guess what. Most every person hates being viewed and treated as if (a) they're a defective person and (b) they're non-unique, non-special, or "less than a full person." Being viewed or treated one or both of those two ways is antithetical to their desire (need, want, drive) to be and to feel unique and special.

All this leads to a certain destructive outcome. When most persons feel or believe they're being viewed or treated as defective and/or non-unique or non-special or "less than a full person," it generates a host of bad feelings in them, including insult and anger.

So, what's the problem with a person feeling insulted and angry? When insult and anger arise, unity and goodwill leave the room — and discord, disdain, and disunity rush in. In short, the main problem with stereotyping is: It's a powerful driver of societal and national disunity.

Moving on, something else that makes stereotyping so destructive is it's invisibly infiltrating every corner of our society without being recognized. It's a foundational component in nearly all the "isms" and "anti-isms" and "social movements" we have today. It's also a key pillar in our news media and, to a degree, in our major political parties and government actions. In short, it's so endemic to our society and life that it could properly be called *systemic stereotyping.* All this is why negative stereotyping ranks as unity killer #1 in this book.

So, if you're a leader in America, please consider applying the powers of your office and leadership role to *identifying and mitigating negative stereotyping.*

Unity Killer #2:
Hate

Hate is: *intense, passionate hostility aimed at a person or a group of persons.* For the past two decades hate has grown within our nation and our government. It has infiltrated and overtaken the minds of many leaders in our government. It has reached the point where these leaders appear to be daily consumed with and driven by hate. Hate would not be a problem except for one thing: Hate is antithetical to unity creation. Hate and unity don't readily coexist. As hate grows, unity shrivels. And, hate within our nation, and especially within our national leadership, seems to have been growing for the past two decades.

Hate combined with negative stereotyping becomes an atomic bomb to national unity. Stereotype-infused hate — or, if you prefer, hate-laced stereotyping — pervades our nation. It has become so prevalent most persons no longer see it — or even recognize its existence.

There's a saying that "a house divided against itself cannot stand." I submit that nothing divides a house more than hate within ... especially when that hate is rationalized with negative stereotyping.

So, if you're a leader in America, please consider applying the powers of your office and leadership role to *identifying and mitigating hate* wherever it arises.

Unity Killer #3:
Vengeance

Vengeance is: *infliction of a negative consequence as a response to a wrong committed.* Other words for negative consequence are injury, harm, pain, suffering, castigation, humiliation.

Vengeance is hate in supercharged mode. It has emerged in the past 20 years in the highest levels of our government leadership. Vengeance is a sucker punch to our nation and its unity.

What's more, following the 2020 election it appeared that there was growing sentiment in our Democratic Party that went something like this: *"Unity, yes — but first we're going to make those Republicans pay."* This reminds me of a popular saying in the antiwar movement during the Vietnam War in the 1960s. The saying was: "Bombing for peace is like screwing for virginity." With a slight variation this analogy depicts what some of the leaders of our Democratic Party are proposing today: "Unity, yes — but first we're going to make 'em pay, teach 'em a lesson, and enact sweet vengeance."

As you likely know, bombing never did make the Vietcong acquiesce or bring peace or end the war. The Vietnam War ended when enough Americans finally realized that pursuing war in Vietnam for the purpose of creating peace in Vietnam was an unworkable, self-defeating stratagem. The War ended when we finally realized that "indeed, bombing for peace was akin to screwing for virginity." And, sadly, this stratagem of "bombing for peace" not only failed to produce peace, it resulted in vast carnage, billions of dollars lost, and tens of thousands of Americans killed.

As I mentioned, there seems to be a notion held by some in our Democratic Party that "First we'll wreak vengeance on Republicans, and then we'll get unity." Is this notion any less doomed to failure than the Vietnam War strategy of "First we'll bomb the hell out of 'em, and then we'll get peace?"

So, if you're a leader in America, please consider applying the powers of your office and leadership role to *identifying and mitigating vengeance* wherever it arises.

Unity Killer #4:
Denigration

Denigration is: *speaking about or describing someone in belittling, derogatory, or damaging terms.* Other words for denigration include disparagement, defamation, derision, deprecation, vilification, smearing, and ridicule. Denigration doesn't always come with hate, but hate almost always includes denigration. Either way, denigration is a unity killer.

What makes denigration tricky to deal with is it exists on a spectrum. On one end of the spectrum is seemingly benign caricature and parody, on the other end is murderous character assassination, *or name-calling at a level of despicability.* Although the former is generally viewed as "harmless humor," we should bear in mind that any form of denigration — be it strong or be it mild — has a strong division-creating effect.

In short, even though denigration isn't as big of a unity killer as negative stereotyping, hate, and vengeance, it's still a nation-splitter.

So, if you're a leader in America, please consider applying the powers of your office and leadership role to *identifying and mitigating denigration* wherever it arises.

Unity Killer #5:
Demonization

Demonization is a radical extension of denigration. It's the psychotic criminal of the denigration family. As the term is used in this book, **demonization** is: *the act of portraying someone as being bad, evil, or diabolic because they voted for a person or a program different from what we voted for.*

For as long as I can recall, up until the 1990s one's political choices, including who one voted for, was viewed as merely a vote, and nothing more. Each person made their political choice based on their best assessment of the situation and the choices available, and that was it. Within 24 hours after the election it "was all history." Regardless of the outcome, there was no great after-vote build-up of animosity, or maligning, or finger-pointing, or blaming, or hate, or vengeance, or denigration. People didn't display hostility or become enemies simply because they voted for different candidates or different programs. Family members didn't attack family members just because they voted differently. Friends and neighbors didn't malign friends and neighbors because they voted differently.

But starting around 2000 that began to change. A perverted force began arising within our nation, and especially in our political world. It was demonization. We began portraying others as being bad, evil, or diabolic because those others didn't vote the way we did. Ironically, the situation of one person voting differently than another person is not what's bad, evil, or diabolic. The actual bad, evil activity in all this is the *act of demonization itself* — that is, the act of portraying someone as being bad, evil, or diabolic because they voted differently than we voted. Unfortunately, this demonization is a corrosive unity killer within our nation.

So, if you're a leader in America, please consider applying the powers of your office and leadership role to *identifying and mitigating demonization* wherever it arises.

Unity Killer #6:
Gloat

Gloat is: *a feeling or expression of great pleasure or self-satisfaction, usually deriving from winning or one-upping or feeling superior to someone, and often done maliciously.* Terms related to gloat include glee, reveling, glorying, and victory-dancing.

In recent years gloat has grown within our nation. It often arises after political victories.

Gloat might appear benign. But it's not. It's a powerful unity killer. What's more, when it's combined with unity killers two through five — hate, vengeance, denigration, and demonization — it creates a poisonous brew that we're drinking daily. This brew is killing national unity.

So, if you're a leader in America, please consider applying the powers of your office and leadership role to *identifying and mitigating gloat* wherever it arises.

Unity Killer #7:
Misrepresentation

Misrepresentation is: *a communication or action that's incorrect or misleading.* Two main forms of misrepresentation are lying and con job. There are seven major types of misrepresentation:

1. Misrepresentation of FACTS
2. Misrepresentation of PRESENT SITUATION
3. Misrepresentation of PAST EVENTS AND ACTIONS
4. Misrepresentation of INTENTIONS or intended future actions
5. Misrepresentation of PRIORITIES AND VALUES
6. Misrepresentation of PERSONAL CHARACTER
7. Misrepresentation of PERSONAL HISTORY.

Misrepresentation is a ubiquitous, slimy unity killer that's so prevalent in our society we don't even notice much of it. But when it arises in news media, politics, government, and government leadership, it spawns discord, distrust, and disunity within our nation.

Of the above seven types of misrepresentation, **#4** — misrepresentation, or lying, about one's intentions or intended future actions — is the most destructive. The act of saying or promising one thing and then doing something contrary is a form of lying, or "con job," that's so pervasive within our government leadership and political parties that we've grown to accept it as "normal" and, so, we turn a blind eye to it. But we shouldn't. This particular form of misrepresentation not only creates disunity it also sabotages the integrity and effectiveness of our nation. It's a dagger thrust into the heart of our society.

So, if you're a leader in America, please consider applying the powers of your office and leadership role to *identifying and mitigating misrepresentation* wherever it arises.

Unity Killer #8:
Propagandized News Reporting

Propaganda is: an image or message that promotes a particular political or ideological aim or slant. *Propagandizing* is: the activity of disseminating propaganda. Which means, a medium that engages in disseminating propaganda is, properly termed, a *propagandist.*

There was a time, in the prior century, when news journalism was mostly free of propaganda. Or, if there was propagandizing it was presented separately from the news reporting in a section clearly labeled "Opinion" or "Editorial." But starting about thirty years ago, various mediums (TV networks, newspapers, radio stations) began injecting propaganda into news reporting. At first this was done subtly and in small doses. People hardly recognized that propaganda was being foisted on them. But in the past twenty years propagandizing has grown. So today we have less true news journalism than we once had — that is, less non-slanted, unadulterated reporting of news events. Instead, much of what we have is something that could most appropriately be called propagandized news reporting. Formally defined, **propagandized news reporting** is: *propaganda intermixed with news so as to cast an aura of factuality onto the propaganda.* Viewed in that light, much news reporting today is, simply put, a propaganda con job.

Propagandized news reporting would not be a big problem except for one thing: It's a polarizing force that's working to disrupt and divide our nation. So, if you're a leader in America, please consider applying the powers of your office and leadership role to *identifying propagandized news reporting* and to urging the media to clearly demarcate its propagandized news reporting from objective news reporting, in a way that readers and viewers clearly know one from the other.

~ ~ ~

(Note: For more discussion on news reporting,
see Transcendence Driver #5, page 82.)

Unity Killer #9:
Chicken Little Fearmongering

In an ages-old fable a little chicken, named "Chicken Little," is hit on the head by a falling acorn and then, mistakenly filled with fear, runs around telling everyone the sky is falling. Derived from that story, the modern meaning of the term *chicken little* is: one who predicts calamity without credible proof that it will happen. *Fearmongering* is defined as: the act of spreading fear. So, combining the two terms, **chicken little fearmongering** is: *the act of spreading fear by predicting calamity, but having little or no credible proof that it will happen.* In America today, and especially in the realm of political parties and supporting media, chicken little fearmongering abounds.

Politicians, political parties, and their supporting media use this tactic in an attempt to scare people away from voting for a certain opposing political candidate, party, or program. Five factors indicate when a particular message or program is chicken little fearmongering:

1) The predicted calamity has *arisen instantly* — it's "big news" today but didn't even exist yesterday.

2) The predicted calamity takes the form of a *"movement"* that's being promoted simultaneously by a collective of persons and media outlets.

3) The predicted calamity has a *political connection* — it's sponsored and promoted by a political entity and the media outlets that align with it.

4) The predicted calamity has a *political purpose* — that purpose being to scare people away from support-

ing or voting for a particular opposing program or person.

5) There's little or *no credible proof* that the predicted calamity will, or even could, actualize into a reality.

Sometimes chicken little fearmongering is so ludicrous it's comical when viewed through objective eyes. Still, it should be avoided. It's presence promotes needless division and rancor within a nation. So, if you're a leader in America, please consider applying the powers of your office and leadership role to *identifying and mitigating chicken little fearmongering* wherever it arises.

Unity Killer #10:
Variable Law Enforcement

Variable law enforcement is: *applying or enforcing a law differently depending on who it is that's violating the law.*

Events of the past couple years clearly show that (a) variable law enforcement is present within our nation and (b) it's a huge creator of discord, distrust, and disunity.

If we're to have any chance of becoming a unified nation, variable law enforcement of *every* kind must be abolished. Laws must be applied the same way and to the same extent in every situation, regardless of who the lawbreaker might be. Doing this, I submit, would have a huge impact in mitigating national disunity.

So, if you're a leader in America, please consider applying the powers of your office and leadership role to *identifying and mitigating variable law enforcement* wherever it arises.

Unity Killer #11:
Hypocrisy

Hypocrisy is: *the act of (a) stating that everyone should be performing certain actions and then (b) not performing those actions oneself.* Or, put more simply, hypocrisy is the practice of "do as I say, not as I do." Or, in simplest terms, it's "failure to walk the talk."

The events of the past few years, especially as pertains to the pandemic, have clearly exposed the fact that hypocrisy is rampant within all levels of our leadership, especially our governmental leadership. This hypocrisy is a unity killer. Our elected leaders should — indeed, must — *walk the talk* ... ALL THE TIME.

So, if you're a leader in America, please consider applying the powers of your office and leadership role to *identifying and mitigating hypocrisy* wherever it arises.

Unity Killer #12:
Schadenfreude

This is a German term that, literally translated, means "damage-joy," or joy derived from damage. More fully defined, **schadenfreude** is: *delight, joy, or pleasure derived from seeing or hearing about someone else's troubles, failures, or misfortunes.*

Schadenfreude is a first cousin of gloat (unity killer #6). Gloat and schadenfreude permeate America today. Schadenfreude might seem harmless, but it's not. Deriving pleasure from other persons' troubles and misfortunes is a perverted emotion. It's also an underlying covert factor that can impede constructive human interaction and unity-building, especially when it's expressed by government leaders, news commentators, and others in position to shape people's attitudes and opinions.

So, if you're a leader in America, please consider applying the powers of your office and leadership role to *identifying and mitigating schadenfreude* wherever it arises.

Unity Killer #13:
Deliberate Disrespecting

On January 21, 2021, the day after presidential inauguration, I came upon a news story of a meeting President Biden had with his staff on that day. The headline of the article read: **Biden to staff: 'I will fire you on the spot' for 'disrespect' to others.** The article went on to say:

> *President Joe Biden on Wednesday warned over 1,000 presidential appointees on a video conference that he will fire them "on the spot" if he hears that they have shown "disrespect" to people in their professional conduct. Biden made the threat as he swore in a crew of political aides who will help him steer the federal bureaucracy. "I'm not joking when I say this: If you're ever working with me and I hear you treat another colleague with disrespect or talk down to them, I promise you, I will fire you on the spot. No ifs ands or buts."*

I applaud that noble initiative. What's more, I submit that it could be worthwhile to communicate that concept to all branches of our government. If shunning deliberate disrespectful behavior is a good move for the administrative branch it also would be a good move for the legislative branch.

Indeed, why do we need any form of disrespectful interaction, even in small amounts, anywhere in our government, and especially between our elected leadership — including national, state, and local leadership? It serves no constructive end. Plus, it's a unity killer that has the negative effect of promoting discord, divisiveness, and disunity within our nation.

What's more, deliberate disrespecting exists within our news media, too. When deliberate disrespecting comes from those who work in government and in news reporting it's a unity killer — and a powerful one at that.

To conclude I pose a question: What, exactly, constitutes deliberate disrespecting? Doing unity killers #1 through 6 — or engaging in negative stereotyping, hate, vengeance, denigration, demonization, and gloat — are perhaps the strongest forms of deliberate disrespecting.

So, if you're a leader in America, please consider applying the powers of your office and leadership role to *identifying and mitigating deliberate disrespecting* wherever it arises.

Unity Killer #14:
One-side-only Characterization

One-side-only characterization is: *the act of characterizing or describing a person, or a group of persons, in <u>one context only</u>.*

For example, describing only the positive aspects of a person and avoiding describing negative aspects is one-side-only characterization. And, vice versa, describing only negative aspects and avoiding describing positive aspects is one-side-only characterization, too.

Further, describing only the accomplishments of a person and avoiding describing failures is one-side-only characterization. And, conversely, describing only failures and avoiding describing successes and accomplishments is one-side-only characterization, too.

One-side-only characterization is rampant in news media and political parties today. They use it to try to create the impression that "their person" is a saintly hero and the opponent is a demonic villain.

One-side-only characterization might appear harmless. But there's a problem with it: It's a unity killer. This happens because the purpose and impact of continuous one-side-only characterization is to supplant reality with fictional fabrication. In short, one-side-only characterization is an attempted con job.

So, what's the reality here? It's this. Virtually no one is all positive and no negative, or all good and no bad, or always successful and never a failure. Conversely, no one is all negative and no positive, or all bad and no good, or always a failure and never successful.

The problem with one-side-only characterization is it's a unity killer. It creates disunity the same way misrepresentation does. Also, it creates disunity the same way deliberate disrespecting does: It offends. It's saying, in effect, you're so stupid I can foist upon you a one-side-only positive characterization of "my preferred candidate" and you'll believe it and, conversely, I can foist upon you a one-side-only negative characterization of "the opponent" and you'll believe that, too. Insult — whether expressed or implied — is a unity killer.

It seems to me that, if one's preferred person is actually the best person for the job, then an open, objective, non-slanted, non-propaganda-driven two-sided depiction of *both* candidates would be the most powerful tactic for getting people to vote for the right person. As such, there would be no need to resort to reality-distorting one-side-only characterization of either the preferred person or the opponent.

In short, a person should get criticism when criticism is due, and credit when credit is due. If all our news media were to adopt that approach it would reduce divisiveness and disunity in our nation, and also increase the likelihood of the best candidate being elected.

So, if you're a leader in America, please consider applying the powers of your office and leadership role to *identifying and mitigating one-side-only characterization* wherever it arises.

Unity Killer #15:
Subterfuge

Subterfuge is: *a deceptive or hidden activity employed to conceal something, usually for the purpose of evading examination and discussion.* Other words for subterfuge are trickery and ruse.

It seems that subterfuge has been growing within our nation. It seems that our political leaders — those very persons we have elected to *transparently* lead us — have no compunction over using subterfuge and deception as a modus operandi. Another example would be some of our educational institutions. It seems that in some schools and school districts there have been deliberate attempts to keep parents and the public-at-large uninformed and in the dark regarding teaching practices and curriculum.

What's the problem with subterfuge? It creates suspicion, insult, anger, and distrust, which, in turn, create disunity.

So, if you're a leader in America, please consider applying the powers of your office and leadership role to *identifying and mitigating subterfuge* wherever it arises.

Unity Killer #16:
Group Extortion

Extortion is: *the act of attempting to compel a person or group to do something by coercing, threatening, harassing, or intimidating.* A contemporary word for extortion is bullying. And **group extortion** is: extortion applied by a *group* or a "movement" for the purpose of compelling another person or group to think or act a certain way.

Extortion in any form is an egregious act. And group extortion is even more so. Yet, sadly, group extortion has been growing within our nation. Why is this? It's because our government leadership and many in our media have been engaging in *euphemizing it.* This has been happening three ways.

First, our government leadership and media have been referring to acts of group extortion as a "protest." A *protest* is: an expression of one's disapproval or dissent. But, when the expression of one's disapproval or dissent <u>includes</u> the act of attempting to compel a person or group to do something by coercing, threatening, harassing, or intimidating, then the "protest" is no longer a harmless protest, it's an act of extortion. Extortion in any form, for any purpose, by any person or group is *bad* and *wrong,* and if it's not already illegal it should be.

Second, some government leaders and media go a step further in their act of euphemizing extortion; they dub it a *"righteous* protest." So they're now double euphemizing it. That is, first they label an act of extortion as a "protest," then they pronounce this act of extortion to be a "righteous" act — whew!

Finally, some government leaders and media even go a third step: they pronounce that they *"support* the right to protest." Such a pious-sounding claim implies that everyone else — meaning, the non-protestors — are people who disapprove of the right to protest. In fact, everyone else *does* support the right to protest, perhaps even more than the government leaders and media do. The thing is, what everyone else does <u>not</u> support is the "right" to inflict group extortion on others who hold a point of view that's different from that of the "protestors."

So, how does group extortion become a unity killer? It creates insult, anger, and distrust, which, in turn, create disunity.

So, if you're a leader in America, please consider applying the powers of your office and leadership role to *identifying and mitigating group extortion* wherever it arises.

Unity Killer #17:
Genetic Sin Presupposition

Genetic sin presupposition is: *the assumption, expressed or implied, that the sins of a person automatically transfer to descendants and family members of that person because those persons are genetically-related to the sinner.*

I'm using the word "sin" and "sinner" in a broad, non-religious context. "Sin" refers to any form of wrong, bad, or undesirable action. And, "sinner" refers to any person who engages in a wrong, bad, or undesirable action.

An example of genetic sin presupposition would go like this. "So-and-so has committed certain crimes. Committing these crimes is a sin, which makes so-and-so a sinner. You are the child (or perhaps the sibling) of so-and-so. This means you're a sinner, too, because you're genetically related to so-and-so."

Another example would be: "Two centuries ago there were slaveowners in America. Slavery is a sin, which means the slaveowners were sinners. They also were white. And you're white, too. This means you're a sinner because you somehow must be genetically related to them. Which means, you must bear responsibility, shame, and punishment for the sin of slavery perpetrated by certain white people of a couple centuries ago."

For two more examples of this concept, consider these.

"A certain member of your extended family is (or was) a rapist, and since you're genetically related to them, this connects you with the rape, which means you must bear partial responsibility for that rape."

"A certain member of your extended family is (or was) a murderer, and since you're genetically related to them, this connects you with the crime they committed, which means you're at least partially to blame for it and also means you carry murderer-type genetics and predisposition."

As you can see, the genetic sin presupposition concept can be adapted to "fit" just about every harmful event or period that has ever happened in the history of humankind.

So, what makes this concept such a corrosive unity killer? It creates and distributes false accusation. It attempts to make a person a scapegoat for something they didn't do or weren't a part of. Being made a scapegoat for someone else's bad actions can make anyone angry. And, being "blamed" for the bad actions of a person or persons who died before we were even born is a division-creating absurdity.

In short, genetic sin presupposition is a conjured fabrication derived from false reasoning and, therefore, is bunk. It's also a unity killer within our nation.

So, if you're a leader in America, please consider applying the powers of your office and leadership role to *identifying and mitigating genetic sin presupposition* wherever it arises.

Unity Killer #18:
Political Gang Blackmail

This unity killer describes two related nation-fracturing elements: political gang <u>vengeance</u> and political gang <u>blackmail</u>. For this discussion, a *gang* is defined as: a group of persons who are pursuing a common aim. And *blackmail* is defined as: the use of pressure or threats in an attempt to influence a person's actions.

In unity killer #3, I described how vengeance is destroying our national unity. This unity killer #18 pertains to vengeance in mega form; it's about *gang* vengeance. If it happens that the term "gang vengeance" rings familiar to you, it's because gang vengeance is akin to gang rape and gang murder — it's a heinous harmful act perpetrated on an individual by a gang of nasty persons.

Shortly after the 2020 election a new trend descended on our nation: *political gang vengeance.* It's the act of enacting lifelong revenge on any person who worked in a particular prior administration. This revenge involves doing whatever one can to prevent that person from ever having gainful employment for the rest of their life. In short, it's lifelong shunning via economic strangulation. I noticed that immediately after the election some <u>companies</u> and <u>organizations</u> began signing on to becoming a member of this gang.

I find this action to be abhorrent ... and scary as hell. To the best of my knowledge, this type of political gang vengeance has never been done before in America.

Besides being scary, it's evil. It should be *illegal;* indeed, it should be declared a major *crime.* Why?

Because what's happening is the starting point for a practice that's actually <u>blackmail</u> — or, more specifically, ***political gang blackmail.*** It's implicitly saying, *"If you would like to be free of lifelong economic ostracism and harassment, do <u>not</u> support, work for, or have anything to do with a particular political party or political party candidate. If you don't heed this warning, we will see to it that you suffer economic hardship for the rest of your life."* This is blackmail at a heinous level. Implicit gang blackmail plunges a dagger into the heart of our democratic process and nation.

Even at the end of the Civil War, which was a time when political gang vengeance could perhaps have been justifiably enacted on political leaders of the South, political gang vengeance didn't happen. Lincoln took giant steps to ensure it wouldn't happen (as powerfully described in his Second Inaugural Address). Lincoln, thank God, realized how abhorrent political gang vengeance would be and how destructive it would be to the future of the nation.

So, in light of this new act of political gang vengeance, which arose immediately after the 2020 election, I ask: *What* is happening to us, *what* are we thinking, *what* are we doing!!!???

Is no one seeing the "what comes next" of this type of act? Is no one realizing that "what goes around comes around?" Is no one realizing that vengeance begats vengeance, and that humans almost always seek to make their "counter-vengeance" more harmful than the original vengeance? Is no one realizing that political gang vengeance on members of a prior administration is about the craziest, most harmful action that could be performed in our nation? Is no one seeing that political gang blackmail is just one baby step beyond political gang vengeance?

Further, how does a person or political leader or political party say, on one hand, "America needs unity, let's put anger behind us, let's join hands and move forward together" and then, on the other hand, promote or allow a gang vengeance vendetta to occur? Political gang vengeance and blackmail is what happens in non-democracy countries, in countries governed by dictatorship and one-party rule — which perhaps explains another crazy thing that happened for a first time — a one-party-rule country signed on to being a charter member of America's first political vengeance gang.

On January 21, 2021, I arose and checked the news. The first thing I encountered was a mind-boggling headline: **China Sanctions 28 Former Trump Administration Officials.** The article then went on to say:

> *China imposed sanctions on Trump administration officials just minutes after Joe Biden was sworn in … [China announced it has imposed sanctions on] 28 people who the ministry said "planned, promoted and executed a series of crazy moves which have gravely interfered in China's internal affairs, undermined China's interest, offended the Chinese people and seriously disrupted China–U.S. relations." … The ministry said the sanctioned individuals and their immediate family members "are prohibited from entering the mainland of China, Hong Kong and Macao." It also said they and entities associated with them are banned from conducting business with China.*

So, to sum up, what occurred was this. On January 21, 2021, the world's largest one-party-rule dictatorship joined forces with the budding political gang vengeance movement in America. At this moment, the gang became an *international* cabal in which its members shared the common aim of wreaking vengeance on American citizens who worked in a prior U.S. government administration. This development is not just bad, it's insane.

As a result, we're now in an epic struggle — perhaps even an existential struggle — with a nation-slaying enemy. And, ironically, that nation-slaying enemy turns out *not* to be some other country or a virulent disease ... it turns out to be <u>us</u>. We are now attacking our <u>self</u>. We have commenced to "eat our own." We've evolved into being our own most insidious enemy. Other nations can now sit back, observe, chuckle, and watch the world's greatest democracy cannibalistically consume itself.

So, if you're a leader in America, please consider applying the powers of your office and leadership role to *identifying and mitigating political gang vengeance and blackmail* wherever it arises.

Unity Killer #19:
Radical Control Programs

As the term is used here, a **control program** is: *a program implemented by a first group for the purpose of causing persons in a second group to perform certain actions prescribed by the first group.* These "certain actions" can be physical actions or mental actions or both. *Physical actions* involve what a person says and does. *Mental actions* involve adoption and application of certain mindset elements, such as, for example, certain thoughts, feelings, beliefs, goals, priorities, values, and so on.

A control program can be for a narrow purpose or for a broad purpose. A narrow-purpose control program would be a program designed to cause persons to perform a certain single action like, say, for example, getting a particular vaccination shot.

A broad-purpose control program would be a program designed to cause a person to perform multiple actions, such as speaking certain words, performing certain acts, and holding a certain mindset — usually for an extended time, such as a lifetime. Put another way, broad-purpose control programs are about "reprogramming" a person from what they presently are into a person who thinks, speaks, and acts according to the requirements of the control program. From here on I call such programs *radical control programs.* This Unity Killer #19 is about radical control programs.

As I'm sure you realize by now, radical control programs hold potential for being dangerous and counterproductive. What's more, they are a powerful unity killer. The upcoming discussion explains how and why this happens.

So how do you identify a radical control program when you come upon one? Or, perhaps more correctly, how do you know when a radical control program is being aimed at you or at a segment of our nation? Answer: You know it by what you see and hear. To assist you in identifying these programs I'll now describe how they work. They tend to contain most or all of the following basic elements.

Elements of Radical Control Programs

The first thing to know about a radical control program is it consists of two groups: (1) a group of persons who are implementing or promoting the program and (2) a group of persons who are the subjects of the program — that is, a group of persons who are the "targets" of the first group. For easy reference, those who are implementing the program — that is, those doing the controlling — we call **controlists** and those who are the targets of the control effort we call **controlees**.

Inherent in radical control programs is a certain dynamic. It's the *Us-versus-Them* dynamic — with the US being the controlist group and the THEM being the controlee group. This dynamic grows and expands through a certain matrix of interconnected beliefs oper- ating within the mindset of the controlist (explained next). Whenever you come upon a person or a group that appears to be holding or acting upon most or all of the following beliefs, it may mean you're dealing with a controlist and their radical control program.

BELIEF #1: Right to Control – The first belief typically held by the controlist is that they have a *right,* and perhaps even a *moral obligation,* to attempt to bring the controlee's mindset and actions into alignment with the controlist's objectives. Connected to this assumption, the controlist holds the further belief that, if necessary, they have the right to use devious, behind-the-back tactics and actions for achieving their objectives.

BELIEF #2: End Justifies Means – Related to Belief #1, the second belief typically held by the controlist is that their desired end, or objective, justifies whatever means are necessary for achieving it. Accordingly, the controlist typically feels free to apply any means available — including any form of coercion — to accomplish the following: (a) cause the controlist's mindset to emerge victorious over the controlee's mindset, or (b) force the controlee to acquiesce to the controlist's point of view or perspective on a certain subject, or (c) force the controlee to perform actions the controlist wants them to perform, or (d) cause the controlee to be "reprogrammed" into the controlist's conception of a right person. The controlist regards any of this as being *justified, proper, and ethical* because they hold the belief that their desired end is so important, or so superior, that it justifies *any* means they might deem necessary for attaining that end.

Accomplishing this can include, but not necessarily be limited to, the following "means:"

(a) Economic manipulation — or attempting to impart economic sanctions or financial hardship to the controlee;

(b) Emotional manipulation — or attempting to impart feelings of guilt, shame, or fear to the controlee;

(c) Physical manipulation — or attempting to impart physical coercion or disruption of the controlee's life; and

(d) Societal manipulation — or attempting to impart societal coercion in the form of hate, vengeance, denigration, demonization, character assassination, shunning, ostracism, and political gang blackmail. Summed up, the controlist believes that achieving their "desired end" even justifies *extortion.*

What's more, it can include attempts at societal restructuring such as, for example, attempting to (a) override or supplant the parent-child relationship and (b) nullify the impact of parental guidance on the development of their children by (c) creating an educational–indoctrination system designed to achieve the aim of installing the controlist's mindset and belief system into the mind of children, all of which (d) rides on the notion that a person working as a teacher or as a government employee possesses more insight than a good parent regarding what type of mindset would best expedite each particular child's personal success and life fulfillment journey.

BELIEF #3: Rightness Derives from Source – The third belief typically held by the controlist is that what makes a particular thought right or true is not any particular aspect of the thought itself but, rather, *where* the thought resides or derives from. To the controlist, every thought or perspective they hold is automatically right or true <u>because</u> it's *their* thought or perspective — that is, it's true because it derives from *their* mind or mindset — AND, conversely, any thought the controlee might have that differs from the controlist's thoughts is automatically wrong or untrue <u>because</u> it derives from *the controlee's* mind or mindset. As a result, the controlist's position is: Any time there's a difference of thought or opinion between them and the controlee there's no need for discussion, debate, testing, analysis, or exploration *because* thoughts from the controlist's mind are automatically true and correct and any deviating thoughts from the controlee's mind are automatically untrue and incorrect.

Now, you might be wondering "How in the world could any intelligent person embrace this type of conclusion?" It's easy to comprehend once you understand Belief #4.

BELIEF #4: Inferiority of Controlee – The fourth belief typically held by the controlist is that the controlee possesses an inferior mindset — or, more specifically, the controlist believes the controlee's intellect, ideas, insights, perceptions, ethics, goals, values, priorities, points of view, and so forth are *inferior* to those of the controlist.

That belief leads the controlist to a certain corollary belief, which is: the controlee is an *inferior human being* relative to the controlist — or, expressed conversely, the controlist is a *superior human being* relative to the controlee. (More on superioration comes in Unity Killer #20.)

BELIEF #5: The Controlee is the Problem – Deriving from the Us-versus-Them dynamic, the fifth belief typically held by the controlist is that the controlee is *the PROBLEM* and the controlist is *the SOLUTION* to that problem. As a result, the controlist refuses to consider the possibility that *they* might be the problem, or that they at least might be a portion of the problem, and also refuses to consider the possibility that adopting at least a portion of the *controlee* mindset might be part of the solution to the problem.

BELIEF #6: Resistance is Caused by Controlee's Defense Mechanisms – The sixth belief often held by the controlist is that any resistance or reluctance the controlee might have regarding adoption of the control program, or acceptance of the controlist's point of view, is caused by defense mechanisms operating in the controlee's mind — such as, for example, the defense mechanisms of denial or rationalization or perhaps both.

At this juncture it's instructive to note a certain point. The controlist's "defense mechanism argument" sits on a table that can be turned 180 degrees and then applied to the controlist, as well. For example, one could posit that the controlist's actions, words, and emotions — or the controlist's obsession with implementing their control program — derives from certain defense mechanisms working in the controlist's mind, such as, for examples, the defense mechanisms of *projection,* or *distortion,* or *acting out,* or *passive-aggressive behavior,* or *reaction formation,* or a combination of these.

BELIEF #7: Controlist Knows the Workings of the Controlee's Mind – Related to Belief #6, the seventh belief typically held by the controlist is that they possess the godlike power of knowing the workings of the controlee's mind — and, in particular, the workings of the controlee's subconscious mind.

This belief is preposterous, of course. It's safe to assert that no human fully comprehends the content and workings of their *own* subconscious mind, let alone the workings of the subconscious mind of *others.* So, why would a controlist assume, assert, imply, or act as-if they know the workings of a controlee's subconscious mind? Here's why.

Fundamental to many radical control programs are certain assumptions held by the controlist. The controlist vigorously protects these assumptions because to admit that any of them might be false would diminish the control program's "validity."

One of the biggest challenges to the controlist's mindset are contradicting statements made by the controlee — statements such as, for example, "I don't hold that belief" or "That's not what I think" or "That's not how I feel" or "That's not the way I view it" or "That's not how I live" or "That has never happened to me." Statements such as these rebut certain basic premises in the controlist's control program and, as a result, they pose an existential threat to the controlist's mindset.

So, how does the controlist keep their mindset intact and prevent their control program belief system from crumbling? They apply a slick 4-part mental gymnastic. They declare that (a) everything they (the controlist) believes and asserts about the controlee's mindset and the workings of the controlee's mind are *true* but (b) the reason the controlee doesn't believe it's true is because some of these mindset elements exist in the *subconscious section* of the controlee's mind, which (c) causes the controlee to be *unaware* of these elements and, finally, (d) causes the controlee to fail to recognize what has happened in their past and what is happening in the present as regards these elements.

Of course, as with the defense mechanism argument, this subconscious mind argument sits on a table that can be rotated 180 degrees and then applied to the controlist, as well. Which leads to this question: "What insidious hidden activity is working in the controlist's subconscious mind that is causing them to formulate, embrace, and promote the crazy notions that constitute their radical control program?"

It all comes down to this. Despite what the controlist might like to assume or assert, the controlist does <u>not</u> possess complete knowledge of the content and workings of anyone's *mindset* and also does <u>not</u> possess knowledge of the development, workings, or effect of anyone's *subconscious mind,* including that of the controlee. In short, the above-described "subconscious mind" contention of the controlist is a self-saving fantasy required for preservation of the faulty conceptual foundations of their control program.

BELIEF #8: Right to Government Assistance – The eighth belief often held by the controlist is that the controlist's control program has a right to be government funded and assisted. Or, put another way, it's the belief that the controlist's objectives and mindset are inherently superior to that of the controlee and, therefore, the controlee should be forced (via taxes) to financially support and promote the controlist's objectives and mindset even when those objectives and mindset are inimical to the controlee's own objectives and mindset.

BELIEF #9: Control Program Supersedes Nation – In some rare instances a certain ninth belief can arise in the mind of a controlist group. It's the belief that the perpetuation and growth of the controlist group and its particular agenda is even *more* important than perpetuation and growth of the nation itself. Put another way, it's the belief that if push comes to shove, the objectives and mindset of the controlist group and its control program must be made to *supplant* the governing laws of the nation, by whatever means necessary, with the result being that the controlist group becomes the permanent governing body over the controlee group.

BELIEF #10: Controlist's Nation Should Supersede Other Nations – In some rare instances a certain tenth belief can arise in the mind of a controlist or controlist group. It's the belief that the perpetuation and growth of the controlist's nation is so important that the controlist's nation must be made superior to certain other nations (or, conversely, other nations must be made subservient to the controlist's nation). Sadly, the controlist believes that their desired end is so important it justifies whatever means are required for gaining control over the other nation — including use of war.

WRAP-UP — Does this description of radical control programs sound eerily familiar to you? If so, it's because radical control programs, in one form or another, for one purpose or another, to one extent or another, have been on the planet for hundreds of years. Every radical control program purports to be serving or promoting some noble purpose or vital need. But they all create antipathy and disunity within the populace, or at least within that portion of the populace that's demarcated as the "them" group by those who are directing and promoting the control program.

So, what is it about a radical control program that causes so much antipathy and disunity? In a sentence, control programs are a unity killer and goodwill destroyer because (a) control programs imply that persons in the controlee group are inferior to those in the controlist group (and for some "strange reason" most people dislike being viewed or treated as inferior to others) and (b) most people resent being told what to do, what to think, and how to live their life, even when those doing the telling purport to be serving or promoting some "high purpose" or "vital need."

So, if you're a leader in America, please consider applying the powers of your office and leadership role to *identifying and mitigating radical control programs* wherever they arise.

Unity Killer #20:
Superioration

This unity killer is perhaps the most pervasive of all. It arises from a certain universal human drive: the **drive to feel SUPERIOR.** This drive is so ubiquitous we seldom notice it and, therefore, seldom recognize how much it motivates what we daily say and do. It exists throughout humankind, and impacts — directly or indirectly — almost every aspect of our existence, including what we say and do in the arena of political thinking and activity. Because the drive is so wide-spread and yet so little recognized, it's often expressed in a way that it works as a powerful unity killer.

To describe how it has been working as a unity killer I first provide clear definition of four terms: superior, superioration, superiorist, and superiorism. I'm using the terms to mean this.

Superior means: *Higher, or elevated in position.*

Superioration (or superiorating) means: *The act of thinking, expressing, or acting as-if one is a superior human being relative to certain other humans.*

Superiorist (or superiorator) means: *One who engages in superioration; i.e., one who thinks, expresses, or acts as-if they are a superior human being relative to certain other humans.*

Superiorism means: *The belief or assumption that one is a superior human being relative to certain other humans.*

(Note: The last three terms — superioration, superiorist, and superiorism — are new words I had to coin for clear explanation of how the drive to feel superior works as a unity killer.)

Directly or indirectly, deliberately or non-deliberately, consciously or subconsciously, each person is striving to somehow feel superior in some way. Each person has numerous options for ways to feel superior. These options fall into two categories: (1) positive superior-feeling options and (2) negative superior-feeling options.

The *positive* superior-feeling options category consists of ways to feel superior without having to cast another person or persons as being "inferior."

Conversely, the *negative* superior-feeling options category consists of ways to feel superior that involve casting another person or persons as being "inferior" or somehow lower, or deficient, or less adequate. In other words, it involves the act of superioration. So, superioration involves two persons or groups of persons: (1) a person (or group) doing the superiorating, which we call "superiorist" and (2) a person (or group) who's the target or victim of the superiorating, which we call "recipient."

Superioration is a pervasive unity killer. This happens because superioration tends to offend the hell out of most persons who are the recipient of it. The reason it's so offending is that superioration connotes that the recipient of the superioration is somehow an inferior human to the superiorist. It's this connoting of inferiority and the offending effect of it that results in superioration being a pervasive unity killer within our nation.

A key aspect of superioration is that it's communicated in many ways — including directly and indirectly, deliberately and accidentally, and consciously and subconsciously.

Another aspect is that it can be communicated by virtually anyone. Meaning, one need not be superior to another person to communicate the impression that they think they are. Or, put another way, one need not be superior to engage in superioration. As a result, superioration abounds — which further means, instances in which people are offended due to superioration also abound.

So, how is superioration actualized in the world of politics? It comes from three sources: (1) From supporters of a particular political party, (2) from politicians or leaders of a particular political party, and (3) from the professional propagandizers, or "mouthpieces," for a particular political party. By far, the most prevalent and powerful of the three groups is the third one: the professional propagandizers for a political party.

So, who exactly are the main propagandizers for political parties today? It's the professional media — notably, the news media. It's TV networks and cable companies that label themselves as news reporters but simultaneously function as propagandists for a particular political party or politician.

Now, it might appear that propagandizing by news media people would not be a problem, indeed not even worth noting. But actually it's a creator of antipathy and disunity within the citizenry of our nation. In doing their propagandizing job, some commentators of the news networks often portray the political party or political leader they dislike in a negative light. In doing this their partisan propagandizing contains unity killers, such as, for example, negative stereotyping, hate, vengeance, denigration, demonization, gloat, misrepresentation, schadenfreude, deliberate disrespecting, and one-side-only characterization. In short, propagandizing news reporting is a major propagator of unity killers.

In addition to the traditional unity killers (listed above), which are infused in propagandized news reporting of our media, there's one other factor that's creating disunity. It's superioration. Some of the journalists and commentators on these networks come off as superiorists. Their superiorist mindset is apparent in the content of their message, their demeanor, their style of talk, and their form of humor or what they find to be funny. All this conveys that they believe they're a superior person relative to certain other persons, with those certain other persons being people who aren't affiliated with the political party that the news commentator is propagandizing for.

Now here's the main point. Superioration action by TV news propagandists and politicians is a *major* unity killer in our nation. This happens because, when we humans conclude, from repeated observation, that a certain person or certain group thinks they are superior to us (or that we're inferior to them), it engenders disdain within us for that person or group. This, in turn, causes us to dislike that person or group. Which, ultimately, breeds discord and disunity within our nation.

But the reality is: Superiorists aren't actually superior. In spite of the stereotypes that superiorist news commentators and politicians might be embracing, in spite of the prejudices and biases they might be holding, in spite of how they might view their self, in spite of where they live, or where they went to college, or the type of position they hold, or how big their salary is, or how rich they are, or what accolades they've received, or what their admirers think of them — they are, in fact, <u>not</u> a superior person relative to any other humans, including those who aren't part of the political party the superiorists and politicians propagandize for. In fact, they're just another imperfect person — no wiser, no more insightful, no more clever than others, and no less flawed, misguided, and error-prone than others. In short, they're not superior to anyone.

Moving on, I point out that one of the things that makes superioration such a powerful unity killer is it combines with most of the other unity killers and, in doing so, puts them into supercharge mode. *Here's how superioration supercharges other unity killers.*

NEGATIVE STEREOTYPING (unity killer #1). The <u>act</u> of negative stereotyping implies that the persons in a particular stereotype category are (a) defective and/or (b) not unique individuals. And this, in turn, implies that they are "inferior beings" to those persons outside the stereotype group. As such, superioration — or the act of striving to feel superior to certain other humans — is a key factor in creating negative stereo-types and negative stereotyping.

HATE (unity killer #2). We tend to develop a feel-ing of hate toward people who cast us in a negative or inferior-connoting light or, in other words, make us the recipient, or victim, of their superioration.

VENGEANCE (unity killer #3). We tend to develop a desire to "get even" with people who appear to believe they are superior to us, or appear to have a desire to make us appear inferior to them.

DENIGRATION (unity killer #4). For many humans, the drive to feel superior is what causes them to denigrate others. By diminishing another person the superiorist creates, within their mind, a larger "superiority gap" between their self and the other person or persons, thereby making their self seem even more superior, in their mind.

DEMONIZATION (unity killer #5). By casting another person or persons as being demonic, it connotes that the superiorator is non-demonic, or perhaps saintly, thereby causing them to acquire a feeling of being a superior person.

GLOAT (unity killer #6). Reveling or glorying in one's victories is frequently an overt expression of superioration. In the mind of the superiorist the win or victory serves as proof that they're superior to certain other humans (or that other humans are inferior to them). This situation can be easily recognized by observing fans in sporting events. When a fan's team wins, that's proof, in their mind, that their team is superior to the opposing team (or that the opposing team is inferior to their team). This generates a surge of animated glee and gloating derived from "their" team being viewed as superior to the "enemy" team.

It's also, for example, why people gloat when their political candidate wins over a competing candidate. Here's the dynamic. In the mind of the superiorist, the win serves as proof that their candidate is superior to the competing candidate. And, because of the superiorist's vicarious connection to the candidate, this further serves as proof, in their mind, that they are superior to the persons who voted for the competing candidate. It's this feeling of being superior resulting from being vicariously connected to the election winner that results in their expression of glee or gloat. Gloaters often make special effort to express their glee in the face of the loser because "in the face" gloating gives them an even stronger feeling of being superior.

MISREPRESENTATION (unity killer #7). One of the main reasons people engage in lying and conning is to put them into a position to appear to be superior to some other person or persons.

PROPAGANDIZED NEWS REPORTING (unity killer #8). A main purpose of propaganda is to make one person appear to be superior to another person. Further, by the propagandist mentally aligning with the person promoted by the propaganda, it provides opportunity for the propagandist to gain a feeling of being superior over others.

HYPOCRISY (unity killer #11). When a person envisions their self as being superior over others that person tends to ignore rules and laws because they envision their self being *above* the law. This implied message of being superior to others and therefore above the law is what makes hypocrisy so offensive to onlookers.

SCHADENFREUDE (unity killer #12). We derive pleasure, and even revel, in the failures and troubles of others because it proves, in our mind, that certain others are not superior to us or, put another way, it proves that we are not inferior to them.

DELIBERATE DISRESPECTING (unity killer #13). We tend to deliberately disrespect others when another person is making us the recipient of their superioration or, put another way, when another is trying to diminish us in their desire to elevate their self.

ONE-SIDE-ONLY CHARACTERIZATION (unity killer #14). By characterizing a person as being all bad, it gives us a rationalization for the notion that we're superior to that person, which makes us feel good and like gloating.

SUBTERFUGE (unity killer #15). When a person envisions their self as being superior over others that person tends to assume their ideas and beliefs are superior to opposing ideas and beliefs, which, in turn, causes them to assume they have the right to employ whatever means are necessary, including subterfuge and trickery, to shut down or overcome those opposing ideas and beliefs.

GROUP EXTORTION (unity killer #16). When a person envisions their self as being superior over others that person tends to assume their ideas and beliefs are superior to opposing ideas and beliefs, which, in turn, causes them to assume they have the right to employ whatever means are necessary, including coercion, threat, harassment, and intimidation, to shut down or overcome those opposing ideas and beliefs.

GENETIC SIN PRESUPPOSITION (unity killer #17). By presupposing that the sins of a certain person's relatives or ancestors are passed on to that certain person by genetic connection, it diminishes that person (in our mind), which enables us to feel superior to them.

POLITICAL GANG BLACKMAIL (unity killer #18). By assuming that another person is morally or ethically inferior to us, or assuming that we're morally superior to another person, it enables us to rationalize an attack of gang vengeance and gang blackmail upon that person. Indeed, one way to look at it is, gang vengeance and gang blackmail are superioration perverted to the extreme.

RADICAL CONTROL PROGRAMS (unity killer #19). By assuming that a certain group of persons is superior to another group, it provides a rationale for the pre-sumed "superior group" to create and implement a radical control program for transforming, or at least mitigating, the presumed "inferior group." And, it also provides the basic concept for the belief system upon which the control program rides.

SUMMING UP: Superioration — that is, the act of thinking, expressing, or acting as-if one is a superior human relative to certain other humans — is a pervasive, powerful unity killer within our nation. Its presence creates widespread insult, animosity, discord, and division. And what's more, it combines with and supercharges most of the other unity killers. And, in doing so it magnifies the negative, nation-dividing impact of those corrosive elements.

So, if you're a leader in America, please consider applying the powers of your office and leadership role to *identifying and mitigating superioration* wherever it arises.

Wrap-up of Part B

So, what do we do now? Sinister unity-killer winds are ravaging our land. *Negative stereotyping* is casting individuals as defective, non-unique beings ... *Hate* is making us want to make our adversaries become non-beings ... *Vengeance* is creating ever-greater hate ... *Denigration* is covering fellow humans with word dung ... *Demonization* is casting fellow humans as evil ... *Gloat* is stabbing fellow humans with a linguistic knife ... *Misrepresentation* is spitting in our face and making us cynical, angry, and distrusting ... *Propagandized News* is making us even more cynical, angry, and distrusting ... *Chicken Little Fearmongering* is making us still more cynical, angry, and distrusting ... *Variable Law Enforcement* is making us suspicious and angry ... *Hypocrisy* is making us even more suspicious and angry ... *Schadenfreude* is making us rejoice over other peoples' misfortunes ... *Deliberate Disrespecting* is creating poisonous human relations ... *One-side-only Characterization* is warping our view of people ... *Subterfuge* is making us suspicious and insulted ... *Group Extortion* is making us cynical, suspicious, and angry ... *Genetic Sin Presupposition* is making us insulted and confounded ... *Political Gang Vengeance* and *Political Gang Blackmail* are perverting our political system to an evil extreme ... *Radical Control Programs* are demeaning us and attempting to strip us of our humanity ... and *Superioration* is casting us as being an inferior human compared to certain other humans.

Given all that, it's little wonder that those twenty elements are creating insult, spitefulness, distrustfulness, antipathy, ill-will, discord, and disunity throughout our nation. I've labeled these things "unity killers." But, truth be stated, they're more than that — they're *nation* killers, as well. So, the first challenge before us is to greatly reduce national disunity by eliminating, or at least greatly mitigating, those twenty unity killers.

Now, these twenty corrosive elements might appear to be overwhelming — especially when viewed collectively. But, they can be easily vanquished. All we need do is cease performing certain unity-killing actions. That's *easy* to do, and the change can be effected in an instant.

So, what does it take to get the process started and then sustained? What's needed is for our *leaders* to set the example — that is, to *walk the talk* and then *talk the walk* — and to continue doing that forever. Sure, this might appear like a demanding, monumental, time-consuming feat. But, actually, doing this requires no more time, effort, and attention than doing the twenty unity killers. Basically, it comes down to the decision to cease promoting certain activities that kill unity and, instead, begin promoting activities that *build* unity (taken up in Part C). For this to happen, our **leaders** must *create* the programs and lead the way to *making* it happen. If they don't do that, it won't happen.

PART C:
Creating Transcendence

The process of creating a great nation involves three main thrusts. First, our leadership must lead us to eliminating those elements that work to divide and undermine us. There are twenty such elements, which are described in Part B.

Next, we must install situations and actions that work to continuously propel our nation to ongoing superlative improvement and life enhancement — a.k.a. transcendence. I call such situations and actions *transcendence drivers.* There are twelve of them; they're described in this Part C.

Lastly, we must preserve, and preferably enhance, the functionality of our nation, which is described in Part D.

So, as the term is used in this book, **transcendence** refers to: *a state of ongoing superlative improvement and life enhancement.*

And, **transcendence drivers** are: *situations and actions that cause one to achieve a state of ongoing superlative improvement and life enhancement* — or, more succinctly, transcendence drivers are situations and actions that cause a nation to achieve transcendence.

Transcendence Driver #1:
Universal Civility

I define **civility** as *courteous behavior.* Universal civility is a foundational component to creating both unity and ongoing superlative improvement and life enhancement within a democracy. This is so because incivility — or rude, discourteous communication and behavior — creates animosity which, in turn, shuts down positive discourse and interaction. In recent years civility has declined within our society.

So, how do we create greater civility in our communities and nation? We identify a certain set of basic actions that we collectively agree constitutes courteous behavior, then we apply those actions in our discourse and interaction with others, regardless of who the "others" are. By everyone applying civility — and, thereby, avoiding acts of incivility — it will go a long way toward creating a productive foundation upon which unity and transcendence can thrive.

One of the keys to creating civility is holding a civility-promoting mindset — that is, a mindset containing assumptions, perspectives, beliefs, and goals that lead to performance of civility-promoting actions, which, in turn, eventually creates a state of civility within a group or nation. Here's an infographic that depicts this dynamic:

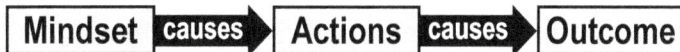

| Mindset | causes | Actions | causes | Outcome |

So, what specific perspectives might be included in a civility-promoting mindset? Here are four for your consideration.

Civility-promoting Perspectives

Following are four perspectives that might help promote civility within our nation.

PERSPECTIVE #1: Humankind is a giant extended family. Every person is genetically, relationally related to every other person *because* we all derive from the same "source" or "beginning." Which means, each person that we see or come into contact with throughout each day is a *family relation* of ours — that is, a grandparent, parent, child, grandchild, sibling, aunt, uncle, niece, nephew, or <u>cousin</u> (including distant cousin). So, barring some good reason for being uncivil to someone, perhaps we should treat others with courtesy and decency because, truth be stated, we're all members of the same family — or, put another way, "we're all in this thing together."

PERSPECTIVE #2: Very few persons, if any, are all good or all bad, or are right all the time or wrong all the time. In evaluating and critiquing others, perhaps we should keep in mind that almost every human being makes both good decisions and not-so-good decisions, performs both good actions and not-so-good actions, does both thoughtful things and not-so-thoughtful things, views some situations clearly and some situations not-so-clearly. In short, very few persons, if any, are right all the time or wrong all the time. Realizing all that, perhaps we should apply civility whenever we're in disagreement with others. It might be that *both* parties are partially correct and also partially incorrect; that both view part of the situation clearly and part of it not-so-clearly.

PERSPECTIVE #3: We stand on the shoulders of our predecessors. There's a tendency today for people to view their self or their generation as being superior to that of their predecessors or prior genera-tions. But this is an ill-informed perspective. Every good thing that exists today derives from or depends upon the lives, work, sacrifices, discoveries, and creations of preceding generations of humankind throughout the centuries. So, we have no valid reason for feeling smug or superior to our predecessors, or for denigrating them. We, instead, should acknowledge the plenitude of good things that exist today that we have because of our *predecessors'* existence, things that positively impact nearly every aspect of *our* existence — or are available for us to *use* to enhance nearly every aspect of our life.

PERSPECTIVE #4: We can learn from what prior generations did, but it defies logic to assume that we would have done anything better or differently than what they did. There's a tendency today for people to look back at prior genera-tions and to "righteously criticize" them for the deci-sions they made and the actions they pursued. The implication of these criticisms is that if they (the critic) had lived back then they would have done things differ-ently and better. And, so, based on that assumption the critic feels justified in demeaning and disparaging the people of certain prior generations.

But is the critic's judgement a logical judgement? The pivotal question is this: If the people of the genera-tion of today were to be magically transported into a prior time and place, and those people had *exactly, and only, the same knowledge, values, perspectives, and life experiences of the generation back then,* would today's time-travel generation do anything differently than what the generation did back then? I maintain: *No they would NOT* — they likely would make the *same* decisions and pursue the *same* actions as the people who lived in that earlier time and place.

So, with hindsight we can *learn* from what prior generations did, we can see what went right and what went wrong, what succeeded and why, and we can apply that insight to enhancing our present-day decisions. But to assume that if we were in their shoes back then we would have done something different or better than what they did, that assumption defies logic and common sense.

* * *

So to conclude this chapter: If you're a leader in America, please consider applying the powers of your office and leadership role to creating *universal civility* within our nation.

Transcendence Driver #2:
Open Civil Discourse

For this discussion, *discourse* is defined as: communication of thought by conversation or written works. And, *civil discourse* would be: communication of thought done in a civil manner. And, finally, **open civil discourse** — a.k.a. open discourse — would be: *the situation in which every person has full opportunity to civilly communicate any thought they have on any particular topic.*

Open civil discourse is vital to the advancement of civilization and especially a nation. This is because it's the process by which (a) falsehood and faulty reasoning are eventually exposed and (b) truth and productive concepts are eventually revealed, strengthened, and preserved. As such, open civil discourse is a road that leads to optimal innovation, progress, and human betterment — or, in short, transcendence.

An opposing action to open civil discourse is *restricted discourse* — or the act of restricting discourse to certain persons, subjects, and points of view. Restricted discourse is a side-path that wanders into a swamp of sub-optimal conclusions and destructive fantasies. As such, it's antithetical to human advancement — or, in short, it's "anti-transcendent." But, in spite of that, it has been growing within our nation. I dub this trend the *restricted-discourse movement.*

Proponents and practitioners of the restricted-discourse movement would have us conclude that the way to create ongoing improvement and life enhancement is to limit and shut down all discourse that's contrary to certain "approved" beliefs, goals, perspectives, priorities, feelings, and so on. Sadly, the growth of this insidious movement is flourishing in three arenas: education, media, and government.

In **education** the restricted-discourse movement exists in all levels and all settings, including, amazingly enough, in the halls of higher academe — meaning, "the university." A mere fifty years ago our universities — meaning, the professorial and student bodies of "higher learning institutions" — were a vigorous, vocal champion of open discourse. So, this leads to a question: Why and how did our universities morph from being vigorous proponents of open civil discourse into being vigorous suppressors of it? Or, put another way, why and how did our universities change from being the bastion of open discourse into being the bastion of restricted discourse?

Also, in the past twenty years the **media** in general, and some outlets in particular, have become active agents in furthering restricted discourse and in sabotaging open discourse. This is ironic. For decades our media outlets have been fervent supporters of the first amendment, even boldly citing it on a daily basis. Yet today many of those same outlets have become devious saboteurs of open discourse, even to the point of actively shutting it down when the discourse runs counter to their political biases. Why and how did our media morph from being vigorous proponents of open discourse to being active suppressors of it?

Also, our **political parties** — when they have control of government agencies — are beginning to introduce government programs that have as their primary purpose the shutting down, or censuring, of open discourse. This is ironic, because for the past couple centuries we relied on our government institutions to be the noble defender of open discourse and also the aggressive warrior against restricted discourse and censorship. Yet, today it appears that even some of our noblest government institutions are morphing from being the bulwark defender of free speech and open discourse into becoming proponents of restricted discourse controlled by government agencies and political parties. Of the three arenas of the restricted-discourse movement, this one is the scariest because it's aimed at sabotaging and aborting one of the pillars of our nation: freedom of speech — a.k.a. the first amendment.

The incursion of the restricted-discourse movement into the arenas of higher education, media, and government is mind-boggling when viewed in historical context. Looking back on prior centuries we see that periods of human advancement — such as the Renaissance — involved an *expansion* of open discourse. And, conversely, certain periods of minimal human advancement — such as the Dark Ages — involved a near-total *shut-down* of open discourse.

Something else worth noting is the historic difference between democracies and dictatorships. Historically, in democracies open discourse has been encouraged and restricted discourse has been shunned. Conversely, in dictatorships, or one-party-rule governments, restricted discourse has been mandated and open discourse has been curtailed and even deemed illegal and punishable by death.

Something else that should be noted is a recent development involving the promotion of the restricted-discourse movement under the guise of righteous-sounding names, under names like "content moderation" and "fake news monitoring" and "disinformation governance" and so on. This trend is dangerous because of three factors.

1 – Each righteous-sounding name for "moderating, monitoring, or governing" speech is actually a euphemism for *censorship.* And, censorship constitutes nullification of freedom of speech. In short, it's exactly what the first amendment prohibits.

2 – For any of these righteous-sounding programs to function it must have a person or group that determines what discourse is allowable and what is censured. Having a government agency or program in which a certain person or group has censorship power is diametrically contrary to what our nation stands for. It's also scary and dangerous.

3 – The restricted-discourse movement and proposed notions for enforcing it ignore a basic reality. If, indeed, a certain person or group has the best conception of a particular subject, or best idea on what should be done, then the best way of validating the viability of that conception is by exposing it to *vigorous open discourse* — that is, by exposing it to full research and investigation, full analysis, full interpretation, full debate, and open publication. This is because, after all the opinions and proposed programs on a subject are exposed to open discourse, the best or most productive opinion or program eventually rises to the top and is the one that's accepted by the populace and eventually adopted.

The reluctance of restricted-discourse proponents to having their ideas subjected to open civil discourse (or their insistence on having "restricted-discourse governing bodies") begs numerous questions, such as the following.

If, indeed, a particular idea put forth by a restricted-discourse proponent is the best idea, *why* are they reluctant to having it submitted to full open discourse?

Are they trying to hide something?

Do they harbor a fear that their idea is too weak to hold up to full public scrutiny and analysis?

Do they believe the only way their idea can ever be actualized is by censuring opposing ideas?

Do they secretly believe that the majority of the populace is so ignorant it can't comprehend the worthiness of their idea?

Do they think that their idea is superior because *they* are superior? Or, do they think that ideas contrary to their ideas are inferior because those who hold those ideas are inferior?

In short, what exactly is the reason why anyone would be reluctant to having *any* idea or conception *fully* exposed to the light of day via *vigorous open civil discourse?*

To conclude, there are two reasons why open civil discourse is cited as Transcendence Driver #2 (second only to Universal Civility). First, it's because *lack* of open civil discourse — or the attempt to exclude certain persons, certain subjects, and certain points of view from public discourse — is antipathy-creating. This, in turn, is unity-destroying ... which, ultimately, is transcendence-killing.

Second, it's because unified direction within a democracy depends on having a collection of optimally constructive concepts that are embraced by the *populace* of the nation. As previously noted, open civil discourse is the process by which that situation is created. Or, put another way, it's the process by which maximally viable, constructive concepts and priorities within a populace rise to the top and become part of the core concepts of that nation. This, in essence, is how unity within a nation comes about. Which is why in this book open civil discourse is cited as Transcendence Driver #2.

So, if you're a leader in America, please consider applying the powers of your office and leadership role to creating *open civil discourse* within our nation.

Transcendence Driver #3:
Informative Political Debate

Public debate between political candidates, especially presidential candidates, has existed almost since the start of our nation. Traditionally these debates were civil and informative. But in recent years that has changed. They're now stage acts filled with false information, false promises, misconceptions, interruptions, shouting down, talking over others, and delivering zingers and laughs. All of that might make for "good show" in the eyes of some. But the end-result is it fails at accomplishing the main purpose of a presidential debate. It fails to equip voters with the information and insight that best enables them to select the candidate that's most apt to perform as the wisest, most beneficial leader of our nation for the upcoming four years.

Viewed another way, the type of performance that results in a person being crowned "winner" of one of our political debates has no correlation to the type of performance that makes for a best-possible chief executive. Indeed, those two behavior sets might be *inversely* related. It might be that the more apt a person is to "win" one of our presidential stage-show debates the less apt they are to function as a competent, beneficial president. Here's why.

The #1 most important function of the president is to make *optimal decisions* — that is, to make decisions that result in being most beneficial to our nation as a whole. And this is where the rub lies. Possessing the skill of "being quick with the quip" and "charismatic on the stage" is irrelevant to the process of making optimal decisions as chief executive.

In short, for our president we don't need a Chief of Zingers and Laughs; rather, we need a Chief of Optimal Decisions. Our present political debates might tell us who would make the best Chief of Zingers and Laughs, but they fail to indicate who would make the best Chief of Optimal Decisions.

So, how might our presidential debates be reconfigured to supply voters with the type of information they need for selecting the candidate that's most apt to make the greatest number of optimal decisions? Here's one idea for how it might be done. It involves seven actions.

Seven Actions for Creating Informative Political Debate

Note: This is submitted as an example for consideration, not as a model intended to be automatically applied.

ACTION 1: Drop the name "Political Debate" and instead use the name "Political Info Session."

ACTION 2: Schedule ten Info Sessions, one each week for ten weeks prior to the election.

ACTION 3: Six days prior to each Info Session, send a set of Info-triggering Questions to the authorized attendees of the upcoming Session. All attendees would receive the *same* set of questions; there would be no special questions for a particular attendee. The questions would change from session to session, except for this one question that would be included in every session at the end of the session: "Is there anything else you'd like to tell the people?" The response time allowed for this question would be one minute, exactly. The response could involve a comment about some other candidate's commentary in the prior week's session, or it could be on any other topic of the person's choosing.

ACTION 4: During each session, each attendee would give their answers to the previously-provided questions from a soundproof booth — that is, a booth rigged so that the other attendees cannot hear what's being said, but the speaker's voice could be heard by TV viewers. This puts all speakers on a level playing field by eliminating any advantage that would be garnered by a subsequent speaker hearing what a former speaker said.

An alternate way of doing this would be to schedule all the attendees to appear at a certain time on a certain day and then privately record each person answering the questions, and then play all the videos later in an evening Political Info Session broadcast to the nation.

ACTION 5: Each of the questions would be assigned a certain time duration (number of minutes) for answering. This time duration would be relatively short, like, say for example, one or two minutes. This short time would likely be adequate for providing a thorough answer, as each speaker would be giving a previously-prepared answer and also would have no interruptions. Applying these times would be strictly enforced. The microphone would be automatically cut off at exactly the specified time, even if the speaker isn't finished, no exceptions. So, for example, assuming that there are five questions involved, and each question is allotted one minute for answering, plus a ten second segue between the questions, the total amount of time each speaker would require would be about six minutes (60 seconds + 10 seconds = 70 seconds x 5 = approximately six minutes per person).

That means, a ten-speaker Info Session could be performed in about 60 minutes. Properly managed, and with good questions, this 60-minute Political Info Session would be concise, non-boring, and, most important of all, loaded with relevant info that voters could use for comparing one candidate to another, and ultimately for deciding which of the ten candidates they believe would be most apt to make the most *optimal decisions* as president.

ACTION 6: There would be a special board that creates the set of questions for each week. This board would be — as much as possible — objective, non-biased, and non-aligned with any particular political party or candidate. And/or, the candidates could submit questions for the board to evaluate and select. Thus, each candidate would have opportunity to have one or more of their submitted questions included during the ten-week Info Session period.

ACTION 7: There would be a Political Info Sessions website. This website would contain each candidate's answers to all the questions of each of the prior Info Sessions. There would be videos of each candidate delivering their answers and also written versions of those answers, all of which would be downloadable.

So, I conclude with this question: How would this process work to propel our nation to ongoing superlative improvement and life enhancement? It would accomplish it by doing the following: (a) eliminating the unity killers that arise with our present "Political Debate" sessions, (b) giving all viable candidates equal opportunity to "make their case" for why they're the candidate who would make the most optimal decisions as president, and (c) providing maximal likelihood of electing the "best person for the job of president," which in turn should result in actually electing the best person for the job.

If you're a leader in America, please consider applying the powers of your office and leadership role to transforming our present counterproductive political debates system into a system of *informative political info sessions,* as described above.

Transcendence Driver #4:
Impeccable Elections

In a republic or democracy the primary leadership is determined and authorized by the citizenry via the process of election, with each citizen having one vote.

When the election process is pure, or free of mistake and fraud, the citizenry has confidence in it and accepts the outcome of each election as being valid. When the process is impure, or containing mistake and fraud, the citizenry has no confidence in it and, as a result, often regards election outcomes as invalid. This causes divisiveness, disunity, and cynicism throughout the populace, or at least through a large portion of it.

So, for there to be unity and cooperation throughout our nation, our election process must be regarded as sacrosanct and the process must be designed so that mistake, corruption, and fraud are impossible, or if not impossible at least immediately detectable and correctable. In short, our election process must be *impeccable* and the citizenry must view it as such.

I don't know precisely what would be involved in creating this process. But I'm certain that it could be created if we put enough commitment and brainpower to making it a reality. Resorting to a trite truism, "if we can put a man on the moon we can (do such and such)." So I say, "If we can put a man on the moon and bring him back again, we surely can create an impeccable election process." I suggest we get it done — *ASAP.*

So, if you're a leader in America, please consider applying the powers of your office and leadership role to leading us to making *impeccable elections* become a reality as soon as possible.

Transcendence Driver #5:
Pure News Journalism

For this discussion, *news* is defined as: factual information pertaining to current events. And, *pure news* would be: news that consists of factual information only and is free of opinion, slant, and news reporter's bias and prejudice, including being free of any of unity killers #1–20. And, finally, **pure news journalism** would be: *journalism that creates and distributes pure news only, and which avoids inclusion of any form of opinion, editorial, and propagandized news reporting and also avoids intentional omission of factual information for the purpose of keeping people less-than-fully informed.*

To achieve a goal of imparting pure news journalism, a news organization should be staffed by editors and reporters who are committed to the noble pursuit of elevating the public mind through creation and distribution of <u>pure</u> news. We'll dub this noble career pursuit *pure journalism* and we'll call those who pursue this career *pure journalists.*

It seems that today there are relatively few pure journalists and few pure journalism sources. Instead, most "news journalists" and "news outlets" appear to be committed to a career of what could more appropriately be called *propagandized news reporting,* or the pursuit of reporting and delivering news in a way that shapes the mindset of others to align with the mindset of the journalist and news outlet. (For more on this, see Unity Killer #8, page 23.)

What's more, it appears that much of today's "journalism world" views a career in propagandized news reporting as being some sort of high calling, and views those who reach the top in this career as being important contributors to our society and life. This viewpoint is at least partially justified because editorializing and opinionating can play an important role in a democracy-based nation. That happens because editorializing, especially when it comes from *all* points of view, can trigger a populace to consider the various points of view and then engage in productive discussion, discourse, and debate. But, nonetheless, that shouldn't be where the greatest focus and highest kudos lie.

Instead, in my opinion the highest calling in the world of journalism should not be editorializing and propagandizing, or trying to align other people's mindset with our own mindset. Rather, the highest calling should be the act of elevating the overall *awareness* of a community or nation through creation and distribution of *pure news* — that is, through news that's free of propagandizing and also free of intentional omission for the purpose of keeping people uninformed.

Moving on, throughout our university world of today there are Departments and Schools of Journalism. I wonder, how many are teaching and promoting pure journalism? How many have a curriculum, values, and faculty that strongly identifies pure journalism as being a distinctively more important function and higher calling than that of editorializing and propagandized news reporting? How many have as their primary mission the training and creation of dedicated pure journalists? I have a suspicion that, if accurately named, many of our Schools of Journalism today would be more correctly dubbed "Schools of Propagandized News Reporting." (I acknowledge that this is my personal conjecture and that, as such, it might not be fully accurate.)

To conclude I pose a question: How would having a greater number of pure journalists and pure news sources work to propel our nation to ongoing superlative improvement and life enhancement? It would do so by creating a more fully-informed, accurately-informed, less prejudice-filled populace. And this, in turn, would result in a populace that's more capable of separating fact from fiction and half-truth from whole-truth. This, I maintain, would strengthen our democracy and create opportunities for ongoing superlative improvement and life enhancement — or, in short, it will help us achieve transcendence.

So, if you're a leader in America, please consider applying the powers of your office and leadership role to increasing the amount of *pure news journalism* within our nation.

*　*　*

Concluding Note: To ensure there's no misunderstanding I reiterate a key point. In suggesting that our nation would benefit from increased pure news journalism I am <u>not</u> suggesting that our present news outlets should be throttled or curtailed. It's my belief that the expression of *divergent* viewpoints and opinions, especially when done in a civil manner, plays a productive role in the ongoing development of a transcendent nation.

Transcendence Driver #6:
Government Transparency and Truth

It's almost ritual. During the run-up to each presidential election the candidates promise, or at least imply, that when they're elected their administration will be transparent and truthful. Some have even been specific; they've promised that when such-and-such upcoming legislation or program is being discussed and debated that *all* proceedings will be video recorded and then shown on TV each night. But it has never happened. And, further, some presidential candidates have promised that their administration will be the most ethical, honest, and truthful ever. Some have even had their members sign "a commitment to ethical behavior, honesty, and truth." But then, as it turns out, the commitment isn't upheld, not even by the president.

All this is sad. And not only is it sad it's wrong. But, worst of all, it's counterproductive. To create a transcendent nation — that is, a nation in which ongoing superlative improvement and life enhancement thrives — we need leaders and leadership operations that function *transparently* and *truthfully* all the time and on all matters (except, of course, when national security would be threatened by public exposure of a certain activity).

Transparency and truthfulness would greatly enhance the citizenry's trust in our national leadership, which in turn would greatly expand our national unity. Plus, it would have the added benefit of motivating our leadership to ensure that they're working diligently to make the best possible decisions and enact the best possible programs.

It's ironic that government leaders and political parties appear to be recently focusing on creating "governance boards" for identifying and shutting down disinformation that arises in the *citizenry,* yet don't seem to be as concerned with identifying disinformation and misinformation (i.e., lies, misconceptions, fake information, false information, etc.) that's put forth from our government operations and *political leader-ship.* Disinformation created by our government is far more dangerous and destructive to national unity and our nation's transcendence than is disinformation arising from the citizenry.

To conclude, if you're a leader in America, please consider applying the powers of your office and leadership role to increasing the amount of *transparency and truthfulness* (and decreasing the amount of cover-up and non-truth) within the leadership ranks of our nation, states, and local governments.

Transcendence Driver #7:
In-depth Action Planning

There's a certain activity that pervades the history of humankind: It's the act of creating desired situations. The typical name we apply to this activity is *achievement process* — or, in one word, *achievement.* Distilled to its essence, the achievement process comprises two parts: (1) the act of creating a mental conception of a certain desired situation and (2) the act of creating an imagined set of actions that, when performed, will result in creating an actual situation that corresponds to the mental conception of the certain desired situation.

We typically call the first part **goal-setting** and the second part **action planning.** The outcome of goal-setting we call a *goal* and the outcome of action planning we call an *action plan.* In any particular area of life, to succeed at achievement both parts must be present. Without a goal the achievement process has no inception and, so, never gets started. Without an action plan the goal seldom becomes actualized — or, put another way, an actual situation that corresponds to the imagined desired situation seldom comes about. (This phenomenon in which we create an actual situation that corresponds to a certain imagined desired situation we often refer to as goal actualization or goal realization or goal attainment.)

When one looks back at the past decades of our national political leadership it becomes evident that oftentimes our national leaders are a star in the arena of lofty, high-minded goal-setting but a failure in the arena of effective action planning — that is, they're a failure at identifying a set of planned actions that, when performed, will result in the creation of an actual situation that corresponds to the goal. So when effective action planning is absent, the outcome is either (a) non-achievement of the goal or (b) eventual achievement of the goal but at needlessly exorbitant waste of money, time, and labor.

Here's a small example to illustrate. Several years ago a presidential administration promoted a particular big-goal public program and congress and the president eventually passed it as a law. The commencement date for the program was about a year-and-a-half down the road. In order for the program to begin as scheduled certain actions needed to be performed in that year-and-a-half period. One of those actions was creation of a computer program for smooth execution of the public program. A year-and-a-half passed, and the starting date for the public program arrived. But the scheduled roll-out of the program was an abortion because *no one had created a computer program capable of handling smooth, glitch-free operation of the public program.* So the scheduled national start-up of the public program had to be halted for a few months so the requisite glitch-free computer program could be created. If the political leadership were to be scored on their leadership and managerial performance, they would earn an "A" grade for goal-setting and a failing grade for action planning. The irony of this situation is: If a leadership/management failure like this were to occur in any well-run corporation, the company president and likely a couple vice presidents would be fired for gross ineptness.

Long story short, achieving national transcendence is impossible without creation and execution of effective action plans for our large national programs. And, it's a responsibility of our national leadership to ensure that effective action planning happens.

Moving on, when ineptness in action planning occurs in certain situations, like the above cited example, even though the cost in money and public disruption can be significant it's not necessarily catastrophic. But today is different. We're beginning to operate in arenas that have goals and public programs so huge that a misstep or miscalculation in action plan creation and execution cannot only be catastrophic but also transcendence destroying to our nation. These arenas include the likes of:

- global climate change

- energy creation and autonomy

- electric vehicle creation and usage

- viral pandemics

- escalating global obesity

- permanent trash buildup (i.e., trash mountain landfills)

- growing drug usage (i.e., growing usage of thought-altering chemicals)

- wildlife and natural resource conservation

- global nuclear war

- massive poverty and starvation

- rising crime

... and perhaps, down the road, unforeseen arenas even bigger and more challenging than those.

Point is, we have no shortage of leaders and organizations articulating lofty, long-range goals in the big arenas. But once these big goals are set forth things become murky. Following the goal pronouncements comes only generalized "strategies" with "arm-waving exhortations" pertaining to how the grand goal must be actualized, but no specific fully thought through action plan is put forth. By "fully thought through action plan" I mean: a plan that is *fully* researched, *fully* detailed, *fully* thought out and that spells out the *specific* actions that must be executed and the *sub-goals* that must be achieved *each year* for the next twenty or so years until the main goal is achieved, and with the plan accounting for *every* aspect and challenge involved in doing these specific yearly actions, including *every* possibility and *every* contingency and *every* what-if scenario that could be encountered along the way. All this may sound hyperbolic, but we're now working in arenas where the situation, the goal, the challenge, the cost of goal-achievement failure, and, finally, the cost of unintended bad consequences resulting from sub-optimal action planning are terrifyingly enormous.

I dislike resorting to trite expressions, but "we need to face reality." We're dealing with goals that require almost incomprehensibly huge outlays of time, money, and public commitment, goals that involve almost incomprehensibly huge unintended bad consequences and public disruption from a misstep or a miscalculation or a "no calculation" or an oversight, goals that — if they're to have any chance of succeeding — *require action plan perfection and execution of the highest order.*

In the past we could get by with sloppy, less-than-optimal action planning. But that's no longer the case. Today, in pursuit of just one of these "big arena goals," if we incur just one oversight, misstep, or miscalculation we could be paying for it in cost overruns and public disruption for *decades* to come. Indeed, in these new arenas of vast challenges and monstrous goals, if we blow it in the action-planning and execution part of the achievement process, the unintended bad consequences could be *as large as* the problem we're attempting to prevent or resolve. So, our national leadership needs to make certain that, as regards each of our major national goals and pursuits, *a full, accurate, effective action plan has been created, debated and publicly endorsed <u>before</u> we dive headlong into that arena.*

So, if you're a leader in America, please consider applying the powers of your office and leadership role to increasing the amount of *in-depth action planning* that's done by our national government.

Transcendence Driver #8:
Optimal Education of Kids

In my opinion, one of the saddest situations in our nation today is the undermining and sabotaging of education opportunity for everyone. I'm not talking about the debatable and potentially catastrophic notion of public payment of "college education." I'm talking about opportunity for optimal education in the most important and impactful arena of all: grades kindergarten through year twelve. Viewed in total context, it appears that as a nation we're achieving a far-from-optimal outcome in this arena. And that's sad, because an optimally educated citizenry is a key requisite for any nation to rise to a level of national transcendence. Now, to be clear, I'm using the term "optimally educated citizenry" to mean: a citizenry in which individuals are, at the least, equipped with fundamental content and application skills in the realms of basic knowledge. And, I'm using the term "realms of basic knowledge" to mean the subject areas of the centuries: reading, writing, math, science, geography, history, civics, and so on.

But today, instead of focusing on the vital pursuit of maximizing educational effectiveness for all kids, it appears that K–12 education has become a political football tossed back-and-forth among politicians, unions, and "social movements du jour" — all for the purpose of furthering *their* goals and priorities but with the resultant outcome of kids receiving a less-than-maximal opportunity to acquire the basic knowledge and skills that propel career success, lifelong income generation, and national transcendence.

So, if you're a leader in America, please consider applying the powers of your office and leadership role to changing our present educational focus from promoting what best achieves the parochial priorities of politicians, unions, and "social movements du jour" to promoting what best achieves *optimal education* of our kids age five through eighteen.

Transcendence Driver #9:
Productive National Mindset

Fundamentally, our potential to achieve national transcendence — a.k.a. ongoing superlative improvement and life enhancement — depends on our collective mindset. Or, more specifically, it depends on the predominant conceptions (priorities, beliefs, perspectives) held in the minds of the populace. This is so because mindset causes actions, and actions cause outcomes.

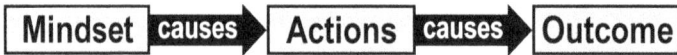

| Mindset | causes | Actions | causes | Outcome |

Effective team leaders understand this three-part "cause-and-effect formula." So they diligently strive to mold their team's mindset to one that comprises the types of priorities, beliefs, and perspectives that will trigger the types of actions that will be most apt to result in actualization of a certain desired outcome — a.k.a. the team goals.

This formula applies regardless of the type, make-up, or size of the team. Meaning, it even applies to a "nation team" — that is, to leading the collective citizenry of a nation to achievement of a certain goal or set of desired outcomes, such as, for example, the goal of creating national transcendence. So, we now come to a pivotal question: What is the specific mindset — that is, the types of conceptions — that are most apt to create the types of team member actions that would be most effective in creating the desired outcome of national transcendence?

To the best of my knowledge no one has ever attempted to answer that question. But, as you might surmise by now, I'm going to take a stab at getting the discussion started. Below is a series of questions.

Answer them for yourself. I believe that your personal answers to these questions will begin to reveal some of the conceptions (priorities, beliefs, perspectives) that are most vital for creation of an optimally productive mindset for *any* type of interactive team, including any sports team and also including a *nation* team.

Team Mindset-creation Questions

For each of the six questions below there are two options — option (a) and option (b). With each question, which option, in your opinion, is most apt to result in creation of an optimally productive mindset within that team — that is, a mindset that's most apt to cause *every* team member to perform the types of actions that will result in optimal actualization of transcendent team performance?

QUESTION 1: Should the team's leadership be promoting (a) the conception that some team members are more vital than other team members for actualizing the team's success, OR (b) the conception that **every** team member is, or should be, an essential contributor to realizing the team's success?

QUESTION 2: Should the team's leadership be promoting (a) the conception that some team members are, for whatever reason, incapable of delivering transcendent performance, OR (b) the conception that **every** team member is capable of delivering transcendent performance?

QUESTION 3: Should the team's leadership be promoting (a) the conception that because the team had less-than-optimally-transcendent performance in the past (season, year, or decades) that means it's a lousy group today and, therefore, will likely continue failing in the present and in the future, OR (b) the conception that in spite of any less-than-optimal performance in the past, or by any former teams, the present team possesses the capability to perform transcendently *today* and in the future?

QUESTION 4: Should the team's leadership be promoting (a) the conception that it's acceptable and okay for some team members to contribute a less-than-full effort in pursuit of actualizing the team's goals, OR (b) the conception that *every* team member should be contributing a full effort in pursuit of realizing the team's goals?

QUESTION 5: Should the team's leadership be promoting (a) the conception that it's okay for there to be divisions and exclusive cliques within the team, OR (b) the conception that "the team is THE team" and, therefore, divisions and exclusive cliques are counterproductive, so *each* team member should be doing what they reasonably can to create a united team in both actions and spirit?

QUESTION 6: Should the team's leadership be promoting (a) the conception that certain team members should be treated, evaluated, and rewarded differently than other team members because of differing ethnicity or gender or skin color, OR (b) the conception that differing ethnicity, gender, and skin color plays (or should play) *no part* in how each person is treated, evaluated, and rewarded.

So, to summarize, for an optimally productive, successful team — be it a sports team or a nation team — manifesting the following six assumptions is essential:

1 – *Every* team member is (or should be) an essential contributor to realizing the team's success.

2 – *Every* team member is capable of delivering transcendent performance.

3 – The team possesses the capability to perform transcendently *today* and in the future, in spite of any less-than-optimal performance in the past.

4 – *Every* team member should be contributing a full effort in pursuit of realizing the team's goals.

5 – *Each* team member should be doing what they reasonably can to create a united team in both actions and spirit.

6 – Differing ethnicity, gender, and skin color plays (or should play) *no part* in how each person is treated, evaluated, and rewarded.

I submit that just as a productive mindset within the members of a sports team is vital for optimal performance and success of the team, a productive mindset within the citizenry of a nation is vital for optimal performance and transcendence of the nation. Now here's the key point. In both cases it's the *leadership* of the team that's primarily responsible for instilling a productive mindset within the team.

So, where does our nation stand today as regards the vital task of imparting productive, team-building conceptions within the mindset of the citizenry? From my perspective, it has been "not so great." In the past several decades we've become increasingly preoccupied with a counterproductive perspective of both human history and the history of our nation. We've become increasingly obsessed with focusing on what's wrong and ignoring what's right, focusing on our sins and ignoring our virtues, focusing on our failures and ignoring our successes, focusing on our backward steps and ignoring our forward steps, focusing on the aberrant and ignoring the good, right, and extraordinary. In short, we've become obsessed with discovering and repeatedly proclaiming all that's bad and negative in our past and present and ignoring all that's good and positive. For ease of reference I hereafter refer to this approach as the "bad-actions approach" to characterizing oneself, one's team, and humankind.

Now here's the next point. If such an approach were taken to coaching and leading any sports team it would degrade that team's effectiveness in an instant; if such an approach were taken to leading any viable, honest business enterprise it would drive it down the toilet in a matter of a couple years. So, why are many in our nation today seemingly believing that this "bad-actions approach" to characterizing our nation, our history, our present situation and our future will somehow create national success and transcendence? It won't. It won't because it can't. It can't because a bad-actions *mindset* causes further bad *actions* which ultimately cause bad *outcomes.*

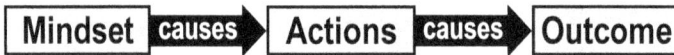

| Mindset | causes | Actions | causes | Outcome |

In short, if we — if our national, state, and local leaders — continue pursuing the "bad-actions approach" to characterizing and leading our nation, we're doomed to failure.

Underlying this counterproductive approach is this rationale: "We must aggressively, continuously focus every day on all the sins and evils and mistakes and bad judgements of all the people in all the centuries of our past, in order to enable us to make our nation and world better today. *And,* we must feel deeply hurt and guilty for all those sins and bad actions of those who preceded us in order to motivate us today to perform virtuously and do right actions." Distilled to its essence, this movement is a *cult of collective self-flagellation.*

The core notion of the cult is that the way to suc-cess and fulfillment — be it individual or collective — is to identify every sin and bad action of the past, and then to denounce and renounce every person who has ever sinned *and then* to daily whip ourselves throughout each day for the rest of our life. And, finally, after doing that — after a lifetime of individual and collective self-flagellation — the sins and bad actions of humanity and of those who preceded us will have been sufficiently punished and atoned for, which then will put us in position to achieve success and transcendence.

While a pursuit of self-flagellation may perhaps seem correct and right-minded to some, it's actually an epic formula for failure — be it the failure of an individual or failure of a sports team or failure of a nation team. Why so? It's because no individual, no sports team, no nation team ever rose to success and transcendence through self-flagellation. As a success strategy, self-flagellation doesn't work! It fails no matter where or in what form it's applied.

So, if you're a leader in America, please consider applying the powers of your office and leadership role to freeing our nation from (a) the "bad-actions approach" to leadership and (b) the growing cult of national self-flagellation. Then, in its place, imbue us with a *positive-mindset approach* to leadership — a mindset that comprises productive, positive conceptions that mobilize, motivate, and equip our nation to perform as a total nation *team* pursuing the goal of actualizing both individual and national transcendence.

Transcendence Driver #10:
Science of Personal Life Enhancement

A summing up of the discussion to this point would be helpful. The ultimate purpose of this book is to describe what it would take for the United States of America to become a *transcendent* nation — that is, a nation that exists in a state of ongoing superlative improvement and life enhancement. To accomplish this, three things must happen. First, we must eliminate, or at least greatly mitigate, twenty unity-killers that presently pervade our land. Part B describes them. Second, we must install, or at least take giant steps at installing, twelve transcendence drivers and also four functionality enhancers. This Part C describes the twelve transcendence drivers. At this point there are three transcendence drivers left to describe. Here's how to view them. Creating a transcendent nation involves achieving transcendence at three levels: (1) at the individual person level, (2) at the enterprise level, and (3) at the national or nation level. This Transcendence Driver #10 addresses the individual person level, Transcendence Driver #11 addresses the enterprise level, and Transcendence Driver #12 addresses the nation level. With that in mind, we now begin discussion of Transcendence Driver #10: a Science of Personal Life Enhancement.

We define a **Science of Personal Life Enhancement** as: *the science of how individuals create desired life-enhancing situations throughout their life.* So, the question now is: *How* exactly does a person most effectively create a desired life-enhancing situation?

In essence, the most effective way a person creates a desired life-enhancing situation is: (1) they identify a *Desired Life-enhancing Situation* they'd like to realize, or to have come about (which would probably be pertaining to one of eleven *Success Areas)* and then (2) they find or create a *Success Methodology* designed to realize, or achieve, the Desired Situation, and then (3) they do the Methodology, which causes a maximal number of *Success Drivers* to be included in the pursuit of the Desired Situation, which results in (4) a maximal likelihood of the Desired Situation being realized, or brought about. Here's this process depicted in info-graphic form.

The Personal Life-enhancement Process

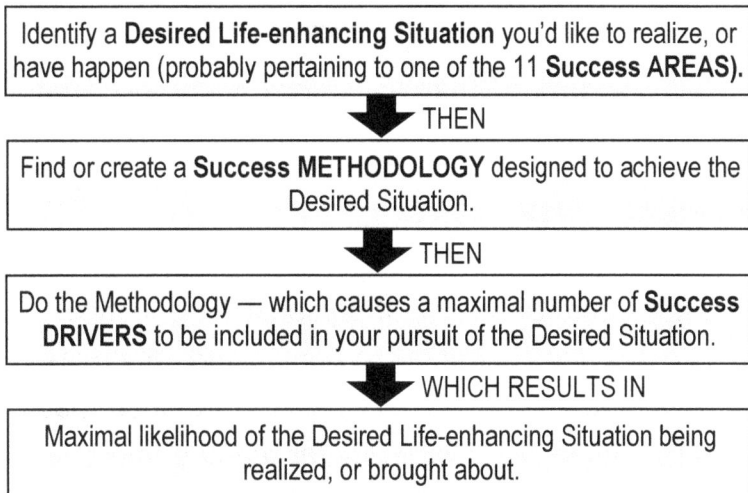

Identify a **Desired Life-enhancing Situation** you'd like to realize, or have happen (probably pertaining to one of the 11 **Success AREAS).**

⬇ THEN

Find or create a **Success METHODOLOGY** designed to achieve the Desired Situation.

⬇ THEN

Do the Methodology — which causes a maximal number of **Success DRIVERS** to be included in your pursuit of the Desired Situation.

⬇ WHICH RESULTS IN

Maximal likelihood of the Desired Life-enhancing Situation being realized, or brought about.

So, the process of creating personal life enhancement involves four key conceptions: Desired Life-enhancing Situation, Success Areas, Success Methodologies, and Success Drivers. Here's the definition of each.

A **desired life-enhancing situation** is: *a situation one desires to have happen, and which, when realized, amounts to an enhancement of one's life.*

A **success area** is: *a basic activity or area of one's life in which life-enhancing situations can be created.*

A **success methodology** is: *an action plan that pertains to a certain pursuit and consists of specific actions that, when performed by a person, cause a maximal number of success drivers to be included in that pursuit, thereby resulting in easiest possible creation of the desired situation or outcome associated with the pursuit.*

A **success driver** is: *a condition or activity that, when present, increases the likelihood of a person succeeding at a certain pursuit — or, more specifically, increases the likelihood of a person performing actions that contribute to creating a certain desired situation or outcome associated with the pursuit.*

We'll now take a little deeper look at success areas and success drivers.

Eleven Success Areas

For starters I suggest that the following eleven Success Areas constitute the range of personal life-enhancement possibilities that apply to humankind. Each area defines a certain type of life-enhancing situation that's within the realm of achievability for many or most persons.

1 – Positive Relationships Development: This success area involves building the number and/or quality of positive life-enhancing relationships in one's life.

2 – Positive Emotions Development: This success area involves building the type and/or amount of positive life-enhancing emotions in one's life.

3 – Flow Experiences Development: This success area involves expanding the amount of time one spends pursuing various life-enhancing aspects of one's life as a flow experience.

4 – Meaning/Spiritual-connection Development: This success area involves expanding the type and/or amount of meaning and higher-purpose in one's life and/or expanding the amount or sense of life-enhancing spiritual connection.

5 – Personal Skill/Trait Development: This success area involves building one's effectiveness in acquiring a certain chosen life-enhancing skill or trait, or advancing one's mastery of a chosen activity or pursuit. This can involve development of a particular physical skill, mental skill, social skill, character trait, or personality trait.

6 – Mind Management/Mindset Development: This success area involves building one's effectiveness in managing certain activities of one's mind and/or creating and maintaining a certain mindset — that is, creating and maintaining certain types of life-enhancing or success-building beliefs, feelings, perspectives, and concepts.

7 – Education Development: This success area involves building one's effectiveness in acquiring certain types of life-enhancing knowledge, education, and/or know-how.

8 – Career/Job Development: This success area involves activities pertaining to finding or creating a life-enhancing career path, or becoming more effective in one's chosen career or job, or advancing in one's career or job.

9 – Avocation/Recreation Development: This success area involves expanding the type and/or amount of life-enhancing avocational or recreational activity in one's life.

10 – Health & Fitness Development: This success area involves building one's effectiveness in creating certain life-enhancing aspects of one's personal health and fitness.

11 – Healthy-weight Success Development: This success area involves managing one's amount of body fat for maintaining one's weight in one's desired healthy-weight range. (Note: A key to succeeding at lifelong healthy-weight living is to make weight management to be a *success process.*)

Nineteen Success Drivers

A main key to achieving success in creating any desired life-enhancing situation is to incorporate as many success drivers as possible into the pursuit of that desired situation. As previously explained, a *success driver* is a condition or activity that, when present, increases the likelihood of a person succeeding at a certain pursuit — or, more specifically, increases the likelihood of a person performing actions that foster creation of a certain desired situation or outcome associated with the pursuit. (Note: a synonym for success driver is *progress driver,* which means the same thing as success driver.)

Here are nineteen success drivers. All of them might not apply to every type of pursuit, but for maximal chance of succeeding at a certain pursuit as many of these success drivers as possible should be included in the pursuit.

1 – Achievement Goal: This success driver involves identifying a desired ultimate outcome pertaining to a particular pursuit — a.k.a. an *Achievement Goal.*

2 – Failure Cause Awareness: This driver involves recognizing the root activity or factor that causes setback — and perhaps failure — at achieving the Achievement Goal.

3 – Success-creation Mindset (a.k.a. goal-achievement mindset): This driver involves holding a mindset of success-promoting views and beliefs, and acting as-if these views and beliefs are a true depiction of reality.

4 – Enjoyment of Process: This driver involves identifying or creating a process, or set of actions, by which daily enjoyment can be derived from daily pursuit and progressive realization of the Achievement Goal.

5 – Motivating Reason: This driver involves identifying the main reason or reasons for pursuing the Achievement Goal.

6 – Mandate Decision: This driver involves deciding that accomplishment of the Achievement Goal is a *mandatory* feature of one's life.

7 – Feedback System: This driver involves identifying or creating a way of measuring daily progress pertaining to actualization of the Achievement Goal.

8 – Reminder System: This driver involves installing a failproof reminder system that reminds one to perform the daily actions specified in one's goal achievement action plan — a.k.a. success methodology.

9 – Goal-achieving Knowledge: This driver involves acquiring knowledge vital to realization of the Achievement Goal.

10 – Essential Actions Commitment: This driver involves making sure the essential success actions for realization of the Achievement Goal are performed each day.

11 – Desire: This driver involves holding strong daily desire for realization of the Achievement Goal.

12 – Focus: This driver involves focusing each day on realization of the Achievement Goal.

13 – Self-communication: This driver involves sending goal-promoting communications to one's self each day.

14 – Progress Tracking and Response: This driver involves tracking one's daily performance as pertains to the Achievement Goal, and providing immediate positive response.

15 – Self-reinforcement: This driver involves delivering reinforcement, such as appreciation and praise, to one's self after daily progress happens, including telling oneself to keep up the good work.

16 – Setback Surmounting: This driver involves holding a productive perspective whenever there's a setback in pursuing the Achievement Goal, and also enacting immediate corrective action and converting the setback into a progress action.

17 – Persistence: This driver involves persistently pursuing the Achievement Goal, and pressing on in spite of challenges, setbacks, and discouragement.

18 – Goal-achieving Relationships: This driver involves discovering and building relationships that encourage and assist one in accomplishing the Achievement Goal.

19 – Whole-mind Involvement: This driver involves having one's whole mind — that is, both conscious <u>and</u> subconscious mind — involved each day in the pursuit of the Achievement Goal.

As previously mentioned, all of the nineteen success drivers might not apply to every type of pursuit, but for maximal chance of succeeding at a certain pursuit a person should apply as many success drivers as feasible.

Note: If you would like to have a "working example" of how the concepts of success methodology and success drivers apply to a specific success area, get a copy of my book *The Key to Weight Success* and read Chapter 3. This illustrates how the previously described Science of Personal Life Enhancement can be effectively applied to success area #11 (Healthy-weight Success).

Eight Activities Involved in Creating a Science of Personal Life Enhancement

As I view it, there would be eight ongoing activities involved in creating a viable Science of Personal Life Enhancement for use by the citizenry of our nation.

Activity 1 – *Identify and pursue an ultimate purpose of the Science.* I would suggest the following Statement of Ultimate Purpose for this new Science of Personal Life Enhancement.

> **The Purpose of the Science of Personal Life Enhancement is:** *To provide an expanding set of simple, proven Success Methodologies that citizens of the United States of America can use for creating life-enhancing situations throughout their life.*

Activity 2 – *Identify and describe <u>Success Areas,</u> and help people identify their most life-enhancing Success Areas.* Eleven Success Areas have already been identified. Over time, additional Success Areas might be identified, and the present Areas will likely be segmented into sub-areas for precision. As an example, the first Success Area (Positive Relationships Development) could be segmented into marital and significant other relationship, parent-kid relationships, family member relationships, work relationships, friend relationships, and neighbor relationships. Each of these sub-areas would have its own Success Methodology connected to it.

Activity 3 – *Identify and describe Success Drivers.* Nineteen Success Drivers have already been identified (in the previous list). Over time, additional Success Drivers will likely be identified, with some of the Drivers being applied to specific Success Areas or specific Success Methodologies.

Activity 4 – *Create and make available at least one simple, proven Success Methodology for each Success Area.* As already stated, a Success Methodology is: an action plan that pertains to a certain type of pursuit and consists of specific actions that, when performed by a person, cause a maximal number of success drivers to be included in that pursuit, thereby resulting in easiest possible creation of the desired situation or outcome associated with the pursuit. Also, it's possible that there might be multiple Success Methodologies for a certain Success Area, so that a person could select the methodology that they believe would be most effective or easiest to apply in their situation.

Activity 5 – *Create a strong official definition of each key concept and term, and compile these definitions into a lexicon of terms used in the Science of Personal Life Enhancement.*

Activity 6 – *Create officially approved validation methods.* These validation methods would be used for establishing the Science of Personal Life Enhancement as a bona fide science. As such, the methods would scientifically prove the validity or efficacy of newly-created, newly-discovered, or newly-proposed success drivers and success methodologies. These validation methods mainly would be used in scholarly research settings, such as universities engaged in doing substantial research in the Science of Personal Life Enhancement.

Activity 7 — *Apply a "science guidance process."* The object of this process would be to ensure that the Science of Personal Life Enhancement evolves in a way that results in maximal positive benefit for the citizenry of our nation. There would be a special board that oversees this process.

Activity 8 — *Enact a promotion strategy for promoting the Science of Personal Life Enhancement throughout our nation.* The object of this activity would be to enhance national awareness of what the Science of Personal Life Enhancement is, what it's doing, why it's doing it, what it's prescribing, and how our citizenry can benefit from utilizing the success methodologies. There would be a special board that oversees and guides this promotion strategy.

As I see it, the above eight activities constitute the essential process needed for creating a flourishing, transcendence-creating Science of Personal Life Enhancement.

I conclude with a question: Why is the proposed Science of Personal Life Enhancement included in this book? It's for this reason. For a nation to achieve transcendence — that is, ongoing superlative improve-ment and life enhancement — the populace of the nation must consist of individuals who are engaged in realizing success at creating *personal* life enhancement.

Without a populace that's pursuing and experiencing ongoing personal life enhancement the creation of *national* transcendence becomes impossible to achieve, or at best harder to attain. So, one of the priorities of our nation should be to create a national Science of Personal Life Enhancement, with the ultimate result of this science being a continually-expanding collection of simple, effective success methodologies that any capable person could access for creating a life-enhancing situation in any of the basic success areas of individual human life.

So, if you're a leader in America, please consider applying the powers of your office and leadership role to facilitating the creation of a *Science of Personal Life Enhancement.*

Transcendence Driver #11:
Enterprise Team Performance-building

For this discussion, we define *enterprise* as: a group of persons that has a legally-defined status and that legally functions as a particular group. The most common form of enterprise is business enterprise. But there are other forms as well, which include for-profit and not-for-profit enterprises. Also, enterprises come in many sizes, ranging from huge to small.

So, we start with this question: What's the main, or most essential, activity an enterprise must implement to achieve transcendence — that is, to achieve a state of ongoing superlative improvement and life enhancement? Here's the answer. The most essential activity an enterprise must implement to achieve transcendence is: *an ongoing process that equips and motivates team members to deliver ongoing desired performance.* Everything that an enterprise does that amounts to a lasting improvement, or a forward step, depends on implementing such a process. For ease of reference we hereafter call that process performance-building. So, **performance-building** is: *the ongoing process of equipping and motivating team members to deliver ongoing desired performance.*

As the terms are used in this book, *desired performance* is any performance that we want to occur. Typically it's any performance that contributes to achievement of at least one of the enterprise's goals. And, *undesired performance* is any performance that's not desired performance, or does not contribute to achievement of any of the enterprise's goals. For any enterprise to achieve transcendence, or ongoing superlative improvement and life enhancement, it must increase, or at least maintain, desired performance.

To explain how to create a greater amount of desired performance we start by disclosing the causes of <u>un</u>desired performance, because the doorway to creating desired performance is identification and elimination of the causes of <u>un</u>desired performance. So here's what you need to know: Whenever a team member or group of team members is failing to deliver desired performance — or, in other words, is engaging in <u>un</u>desired performance — it's always because one or more of these four conditions exists:

1 – LACK OF AWARENESS of what action and outcomes constitute desired performance;

2 – LACK OF ABILITY to do desired performance;

3 – LACK OF RESOURCES to do desired performance; or

4 – LACK OF MOTIVATION to do desired performance.

Those four conditions are the *four causes of undesired performance.* They are the *only* causes of undesired performance. Whenever a person or group is failing to create desired performance it's always because one or more of those four factors is at work. So, to eliminate a situation of repetitive undesired performance one must identify the cause of the undesired performance and replace it with its opposite, which we hereafter refer to as a Requisite for Desired Performance. So, since there are four causes of undesired performance, that means there are four requisites to desired performance. They are:

1 – **A**WARENESS of what action and outcomes constitute Desired Performance.

2 – **A**BILITY to do desired performance.

3 – **R**ESOURCES to do desired performance.

4 – **M**OTIVATION to do desired performance.

You'll note that the *four requisites to desired performance* are the "opposites" of the four causes of undesired performance. When awareness, ability, resources, and motivation are present, desired performance *happens.* Whenever desired performance is not happening, it means one or more of the four requisites is *missing.* These four requisites are the four pieces of the performance-building paradigm. To remember them, think of AARM. And bear in mind that providing these four pieces is how we "AARM" team members to accomplish desired performance.

So, how does one create the four requisites for desired performance? One does it by applying four activities that create the four requisites. We refer to these four activities as the *four functions for creating desired performance*. They are:

1 – DESCRIBING desired performance;

2 – TRAINING for desired performance;

3 – EQUIPPING for desired performance;

4 – MOTIVATING for desired performance.

When these four functions for creating desired performance properly occur, the four requisites are created and, in turn, desired performance *happens.* Conversely, when any of these four functions has <u>not</u> occurred, usually at least one of the four requisites will be missing or deficient and, accordingly, desired performance will *not* have happened. The above discussion discloses, in a nutshell, the "secret" of performance-building.

The next step in this subject involves explanation of how an enterprise can install the four functions for creating desired performance. At this point the discussion goes beyond the size and scope of this book you're right now reading. To continue the discussion later, for those enterprise leaders who might be interested in pursuing it, I'm presently in process of creating a book that describes in detail how to create and manage those four functions for creating desired performance in any enterprise. I'm aiming to have the book published by end of 2024 or in the first half 2025.

But, in case you might be interested in immediately delving into the subject of motivating team members, you might check out my book titled *Motivate.* It's a short read — yet powerful.

So, for now I wrap up this discussion of Transcendence Driver #11, but I reiterate that enterprise team performance-building is a vital aspect to bringing transcendence to our nation. So, please, leaders in America — whoever you are, wherever you might be — lead us to facilitating the creation of *Enterprise Team Performance-building* throughout America. Doing this will make our nation stronger and a better place in which to live.

Transcendence Driver #12:
Unity-creating Leadership

For this discussion, *unity* is defined as: a situation in which multiple persons are working harmoniously together toward realization of a common purpose and goals.

To eliminate the unity killers pervading our nation today and also to begin installing transcendence drivers nationwide, we must have **unity-creating leadership.** That is, we must have leaders who lead our nation to *unity* and also to *transcendence.*

This was the case even at the start of our nation. Our union arose by acts of unity-creating leadership. Certain leaders of that time, such as Benjamin Franklin for example, created and promoted solutions and concepts that resolved seemingly intractable disagreements and disunity among the thirteen original colonies. As a result of these unity-creating concepts (which included the concept of a bicameral legislature) it enabled the thirteen colonies to come together and form a single nation. In short, without acts of unity-creating leadership our nation would likely not exist today.

Not surprisingly, we still have a huge need for unity-creating leadership even today. For example, it would appear that the "pro-life vs. pro-choice battle" is a seemingly intractable disagreement, one that appears so divisive that it could tear us apart, or at least greatly reduce our efforts at creating national transcendence.

But is this disagreement unsolvable? Meaning, is there no way of moving beyond this seeming impasse and into a territory in which we can function civilly and in unity? To achieve that, I suggest that two things need to happen. First, we need to recognize that the first priority — a priority above all others — is to preserve the nation. I say this because fracturing or dissolving the nation is a non-solution. Without a full-functioning nation we lose — both collectively and individually — nearly every good thing we have today (more coming up on this in Part D).

Second, to create a solution we need unity-creating leadership to step forward and initiate a process for identifying a workable program that would be mutually acceptable to both parties. By "mutually acceptable to both parties" I don't mean "perfect in the eyes of each party." It's not likely that it would be possible at this time to craft a solution that's perfect in the eyes of both parties. But, I believe that with the right leadership — i.e., unity-creating leadership — it would be possible to create and implement a solution that would be "good enough" for each of the two sides to accept at this time, and thereby enable our nation to extinguish the firestorm of unity killers that has been attending the "pro-life versus pro-choice battle." This, then, would enable our nation to move forward on a track of national unity and transcendence.

To conclude, it might be that the final words in the last public speech by Patrick Henry, in 1799, are applicable to the situation today. At that time there were seemingly intractable issues that were threatening to tear apart the infant nation. Patrick Henry presciently advised:

> "Let us trust God, and our better judgment, to set us right hereafter. United we stand, divided we fall. Let us not split into factions which must destroy that union upon which our existence hangs."

It seems that our nation today has a plethora of "unity-destroying leaders" — leaders who allow, endorse, promote, and at times even contribute to the unity-killers firestorm that's presently ravaging our land. This is bad and sad. We can no longer afford to continue squandering time and resources on pursuing parochial priorities that create disunity and thwart transcendence. For the future, our nation needs leadership that's focused on making decisions and instituting actions that are most effective at *building* unity and transcendence in our nation.

So, if you're a leader in America, please consider applying the powers of your office and leadership role to facilitating the identification and election of *unity-creating leadership* for the top levels of our national and state governments. If it happens that you're one who aspires to be a unity-creating leader, then sharpen your unity-creating leadership skills to the max, and "give it a go" at election time. But, on the other hand, if you recognize that there are other persons who have stronger unity-creating leadership skills than you, then step aside and urge those persons to step forward and fulfill our nation's present need for unity-creating leadership.

PART D:
Enhancing Our Nation's Functionality

There's something critical that we, the citizenry of the United States of America, must recognize: Nearly every good thing we have, in one way or another, to one extent or another, derives from and depends upon the *functionality* of our nation. Meaning, if our nation were to somehow become "dis-united" or less-than-fully-functional, most of the good things we enjoy in our life — things that most of us take for granted — would greatly decline or disappear. In short, the continuation and advancement of the positive elements of our existence ride on continued improvement in the functionality of our nation. For this discussion I define **functionality** as: *the capability to function in a way that achieves a certain desired outcome.*

So, in addition to building unity and transcendence (described in Parts B and C) we also must preserve and enhance our nation's functionality. To aid in doing that, following are four suggestions that, when applied, would result in strengthening our nation's functionality. I dub them *functionality enhancers.*

Functionality Enhancer #1:
Functionalized Strategic Plans

The realm of management can be divided into two parts: real-time management and strategic management. Real-time management — sometimes called tactical management — includes activities involved in managing a situation that requires immediate, hourly, or daily attention. Strategic management, on the other hand, includes activities involved in devising and executing plans aimed at achieving certain desired outcomes in the future, oftentimes years in the future. These "certain desired outcomes at some time in the future" we call *strategic goals.* The process of creating the plans for achieving the strategic goals we call *strategic planning* and the result of the planning we call a *strategic plan.*

In creating strategic plans government leaders and groups sometimes compile impressive lists of activities that could be effective in actualizing the strategic goal. But, in their zeal of pursuing the strategic goal they end up with a strategic plan that's a timebomb to our nation's functionality — that is, they end up with a plan that, when implemented, will result in degrading or destroying our nation's strength and quality of life.

To avoid such a disaster, our government leaders must ensure that each strategic plan is structured in such a way that, when implemented, it *preserves* our nation's functionality at all times. For this discussion, we're calling such a plan a **functionalized strategic plan.**

Why are functionalized strategic plans essential? It's because if we lose national functionality during the near-term phase or during the mid-term phase of executing a strategic plan, the noble strategic goal that's expected to be realized during the long-term phase becomes inconsequential — because as a nation we'll be either *minimally functional* or *non-existent* by that time.

So, if you're a leader in America, please consider applying the powers of your office and leadership role to facilitating the creation of *functionalized strategic plans* — plans that, when implemented, preserve our nation's functionality, strength, and quality of life *at all times.*

Functionality Enhancer #2:
Effective Real-time Management

As previously explained, there are two types of management: strategic management and real-time management. We use strategic management for actualizing strategic goals. We use real-time management — which we're now calling *effective* real-time management — for managing situations requiring immediate attention. For this discussion, we define **effective real-time management** as: *the act of effectively directing immediate, hourly, or daily action to the management of a situation that requires immediate, hourly, or daily attention.*

One of the seeming hang-ups in the world of government leadership is that sometimes our leaders misapply these two types of management. That is, they sometimes apply real-time management action to a situation that calls for strategic management action and, conversely, they apply strategic management action to a situation that calls for effective real-time management action. I'll illustrate with a hypothetical example: a big 30-story apartment building is on fire. The fire is raging and growing. Which type of response should the leaders of the fire department apply to this situation? They have two options.

The first possible response would be to apply a *strategic management approach.* For this, the fire chief would convene a meeting of the staff to discuss important aspects of fires and fire prevention. The group might decide that the top priority is to organize exploratory studies of various factors related to fires and especially apartment fires. The noble purpose of these studies might include: (a) gathering research on the frequency of apartment building fires in the past couple years, (b) studying the causes of apartment building fires, including both the immediate causes and the root causes, (c) conferring with fire departments of other cities to find out what they've been doing to reduce the frequency of apartment building fires, (d) doing an analysis of social and demographic data to determine if there's a correlation between apartment building fires and demographic factors such as income, job types, educational background, race, gender, and so on, (e) conducting research on fire prevention systems best used in apartment buildings, (f) drafting a request for a major increase in fire department budget and staff for the upcoming fiscal year, (g) calling for the legislature to draft legislation to make fire prevention to be in the required curriculum in high schools, and (h) begin a publicity campaign, including social media and TV appearances, to ensure that the fire department in no way carries any responsibility for the fire now raging in the apartment building.

The second possible response would be to apply an *effective real-time management approach.* With this, the fire chief and staff immediately jump into action to manage the firefighting effort at the apartment building and to ensure maximal effectiveness in fighting the fire. They take command of the situation. They issue orders and communications in real time, constantly assessing and reassessing the situation, reallocating firefighter personnel as needed for optimal impact. If needed, they call nearby fire departments to gain additional firefighting resources. In short, they commit total focus on the goal of extinguishing the fire as soon as possible; they don't let anything interrupt their effort until that outcome is achieved.

So, which management response should the fire chief and staff adopt for this situation? Obviously, the second one — the situation is something that calls for immediate action and real-time attention.

Now, how does this apply to our government leadership? Sometimes our government leaders seem to hesitate or become confused about which approach to apply to a certain situation. In some cases we've had a situation that calls for immediate, hourly, and/or daily attention but our leaders seem to be adopting a strategic management approach, or some approach other than effective real-time management of the situation. Now, in saying that, I acknowledge that this is how it appears from my perspective. If that perspective happens to be incorrect, I stand corrected. I'll let you, the reader, determine whether this perspective is valid or not.

Functionality Enhancer #3:
Superior Managerial Skills

After 78 years of being an American citizen, I've concluded that it's not uncommon to have a person of less-than-optimal managerial effectiveness heading up a vital department, bureau, agency, or other important government component. Perhaps I've been misinterpreting the situation from my limited perspective. And, if I have, I stand corrected. But, on the other hand, if my perspective happens to be an accurate view of the situation, then one of the most powerful actions our nation could take for creating *optimal functionality* in our nation would be: Institute a program that *ensures* that *every* key managerial position in our government is staffed with a head manager who possesses *superior* managerial skills and effectiveness.

The functioning of our government bodies has become so large, complex, and impactful that we can no longer "cruise along" with average or "good enough" or less-than-the-best managerial performance. To minimize the chance of managerial malfunction and calamity, we need to staff our government bodies with top managers of the *highest* caliber possible and who possess *superior* managerial skills and effectiveness.

So, if you're a leader in America, please consider applying the powers of your office and leadership role to facilitating the creation of a program that ensures that the leadership positions of our governmental bodies — both national and state — are staffed with persons possessing *superior managerial skills and effectiveness.*

Functionality Enhancer #4:
Nation Before Party

Frequently our elected national leaders are faced with a certain type of situation. They face a decision involving two mutually exclusive choices, which we'll label (a) and (b). Choice (a) promotes the priorities of the nation, choice (b) promotes the priorities of the person's political party or their self. And, as previously stated, the choices are mutually exclusive — both cannot be achieved at the same time.

Naturally, since the person was elected by the citizenry to serve in the capacity of a national leader, one would expect that the person would vote for choice (a). But, all too often, they instead vote for choice (b). This can be sad, because even though choice (b) might promote the "functionality" of the party or of the political leader, it often *diminishes* the functionality of the nation. And, a decision or action that diminishes the functionality of the nation is a bad thing to have happen. So, it might be good for our nation if the top leadership of our nation were to more often put "Nation before Party" when making decisions that impact our nation.

PART E:
What Should We Be Doing Now?

So, what might all this portend for the future? I submit that it involves three questions.

QUESTION #1: What should be our nation's top priorities?

I maintain that our nation should have three top priorities: Unity, Transcendence, Functionality — described as this.

PRIORITY 1: **Create Unity** — that is, cause the citizenry of our nation to turn away from unity-killing activities (described in Part B) and, instead, unite and begin working harmoniously together toward realization of common purpose and goals.

PRIORITY 2: **Create Transcendence** — that is, create ongoing superlative improvement and life enhancement within our nation. A first step to accomplishing this is to install transcendence drivers (described in Part C).

PRIORITY 3: **Enhance our nation's Functionality** — that is, enhance our nation's capability to function in a way that achieves a certain desired outcome or way of life, including unity and transcendence. A first step to accomplishing this is to install functionality enhancers (described in Part D). Plus, it also involves protecting our nation from external threats and also internal entropy (i.e., crime, chaos, drugs, destruction, etc.).

So, in a nutshell, the three top priorities of our nation should be: *Unity, Transcendence,* and *Functionality.*

QUESTION #2: What should be the top priorities of our leaders?

Since the top three priorities of our nation should be Unity, Transcendence, and Functionality, those also should be the top three priorities of our leadership, especially our national and state leadership.

QUESTION #3: Are the leaders of our nation providing the best possible leadership?

This is a question we should be asking ourself every year, all the time. We should be doing this because this is a pivotal question, a question of existential impact, a question the answer of which determines the destiny of our nation and, therefore, the destiny of the individual citizens constituting our nation both today and in the future. If the answer turns out to be "Yes" then America and its citizens will likely be in good shape in the years to come. But, if the answer turns out to be "No" then we and our descendants could be in for numerous decades of tough travel.

So it comes down to this. Everything in our future rides on the *wisdom and effectiveness of our leadership*. More than any other factor, the leadership of America is what will be determining the fate of America. In short, to succeed and thrive over the long term, our leadership must be the *wisest, most effective* leadership that's possible to have. Everything comes down to that. Effective leadership = good future; not-so-effective leadership = not-so-good future.

To bring the matter into focus, here are a few examples of corollary questions to that main pivotal question (#3 above).

1 – Are our leaders doing the best possible job of *unifying* America's citizenry? (If they're not, we need to replace them with new leaders!)

2 – Are our leaders doing the best possible job of leading America to *transcendence* — that is, to ongoing superlative improvement and life enhancement?

3 – Are our leaders doing the best possible job of enhancing America's *functionality* — that is, enhancing our capability to achieve the type of positive lifestyle we desire to be living?

4 – Are our leaders doing the best possible job of *motivating* America's citizenry to higher performance?

5 – Are our leaders doing the best possible job of setting *productive, inspiring national goals?*

6 – Are our leaders doing the best possible job of creating *effective, functional action plans* for America?

7 – Are our leaders doing the best possible job of *managing our economy?*

8 – Are our leaders doing the best possible job of ensuring an *optimal K–12 education system* for America?

9 – Are our leaders doing the best possible job of *protecting our nation* from external threats?

10 – Are our leaders doing the best possible job of *reducing internal entropy* (i.e., crime, chaos, drugs, destruction, etc.)?

11 – Are our leaders doing the best possible job of ensuring that departments in our national and state government are being led by managers who possess *superior managerial skills and effectiveness?*

12 – Are our leaders doing the best possible job of putting our *nation's priorities* before their own personal and political party priorities?

IN SHORT, the future of our nation rides on the wisdom and effectiveness of the *leadership* of our nation. Lousy leading = lousy future; mediocre leading = mediocre future; great leading = great future. Everything comes down to that.

Now, I am <u>not</u> posing questions like these in light of any particular president or administration or congressional session. As I see it, we should be asking ourself these types of questions *every* year and pertaining to *every* set of leaders we have. We should be doing it because the future of our nation, and therefore the future of the individual citizens of our nation, are riding on the answers to those questions.

So, referring back to the *Open Letter to President Biden and Subsequent Presidents, and Also to All the Other Leaders in America* (p. 3), if America is going to "put the anger and the harsh rhetoric behind us and come together as a nation," the only way that that's going to happen is if our *leadership performs actions that <u>make</u> it happen!* Which is to say, the only way the citizenry of America is going to achieve unity is by our leadership *leading* us to unity.

For the past several decades a certain style of leadership has arisen in America. It's a style that has been fostering unity-killer activity galore along with all the attendant negative outcomes that result from that activity (described in Part B). I suggest that we should set this style of leadership aside. In its place we should bring in a new style of leading, a style that works to *mitigate* unity killers and strengthen *unity creation* and, at the same time, increase transcendence and functionality of our nation. We should be doing this because the future of our nation depends on us succeeding at doing it.

We also face some haunting questions, such as: *What will the America of tomorrow be like?* Will it be a place that continues to be riddled with ever-hardening, diametrically-opposing, mutually-exclusive attitudes and perspectives, <u>OR</u> will it be a place where people — and in particular our leaders — step out of their bunkers and onto a space in the middle, and begin jointly, diligently working at creatively crafting *unifying* solutions to strongly-held divergent points of view, solutions that may not be perfect from every point of view but which are, in the eyes of most people, at least "good enough for the present," and that, thereby, enable our nation to push aside the corrosive unity killers and growing divisiveness that have been plaguing our nation, and in their place, begin expanding unity, civility, and positive interactions throughout our society and nation, and thereby take our nation off the old road of unity killers, divisiveness, and discord, and onto a new road of ever-expanding unity, transcendence, and optimal functionality?

Now, to begin wrapping up this book — first, I thank you for reading it. Then I cite these closing lines from Lincoln's immortal Gettysburg Address during the Civil War — words that remain poignant to the present day:

... that we here highly resolve that these dead shall not have died in vain — that this nation, under God, shall have a new birth of freedom — and that government of the people, by the people, for the people, shall not perish from the earth.

Now one of my favorite photos ...

What Now, America?

THREE BASIC PRECEPTS REQUIRED FOR OUR NATION'S SUCCESS

1 – For most good things to come about, we need OPTIMAL FUNCTIONALITY of the Nation.

2 – For Optimal Functionality of the Nation, we need UNITY.

3 – To get Unity, we must inform our Leaders that creating Unity is MANDATORY. <u>This</u> is the *Key.*

Definitions

Optimal functionality is: the capability to function in a way that achieves a certain desired outcome, such as, for example, a certain desired way of life.

Unity is: people working harmoniously together toward realization of common purpose and goals, such as, for example, the goal of realizing ongoing superlative improvement and life enhancement — a.k.a. transcendence.

Mandatory means: something that must be done in order for a person to keep their job.

This is the last page of this book —
it's now time for America to

UNITE

With **Unity** we will Stand,
without it we will Fall.

With **Transcendence** we will Rise,
without it we will Decline.

With optimal **Functionality** we will Prosper,
without it we will Wither.

More than any other factor, the *words and actions of
our leadership* determine whether we do, or do not,
achieve Unity, Transcendence, and optimal
Functionality.

www.ingramcontent.com/pod-product-compliance
Lightning Source LLC
Chambersburg PA
CBHW080758300326
41914CB00055B/938